The
Little Notebook

The Journal of a
Contemporary Woman's Encounters
with Jesus

❶

NICOLE GAUSSERON

Translated and Edited by
William Skudlarek and Hilary Thimmesh

HarperSanFrancisco
A Division of HarperCollins*Publishers*

FIRST EDITION

Library of Congress Cataloging-in-Publication Data:
Gausseron, Nicole
The little notebook : the journal of a contemporary woman's encounters with Jesus / Nicole Gausseron : translated from the French and edited by William Skudlarek and Hilary Thimmesh. — 1st ed.
p.   cm.
ISBN 0–06–063099–X (alk. paper)
1. Gausseron, Nicole—Diaries. 2. Catholics—France—Diaries. 3. Visions. 4. Jesus Christ—Apparitions and miracles—France—Chartres. 5. Compagnons du Partage. 6. Church work with the homeless—France—Chartres. 7. Chartres (France)—Church history—20th century. I. Skudlarek, William. II. Thimmesh, Hilary. III. Title.
BX4705.G2636A3   1995
282'.092—dc20
[B]   94–42561
                                                              CIP

94 95 96 97 98 ❖ RRD(H) 10 9 8 7 6 5 4 3 2 1

This edition is printed on acid-free paper that meets the American National Standards Institute Z39.48 Standard.

Contents

Foreword

by Joseph F. Girzone

Ordinarily, I have a strong negative reaction to books purporting to record the author's dialogues with God or the Blessed Virgin or other celestial beings. But there was something about this book that fascinated me after reading only a few pages. It was not the usual pious saccharin so common to books of this type. The personality of Nicole was too earthy and too apparently disrespectful to be concocted. It certainly was not recorded to impress anyone.

As I read on I began to think of my childhood. For a period of perhaps five years, from age eleven to sixteen, I experienced an intimacy with God similar to that which Nicole writes about so poignantly. I knew God was close. I knew He was guiding me and the intimacy of the experience indelibly impressed upon my mind the reality of God. Then when I was sixteen years old it came to an abrupt end, never to return. I know it is a phase in the deepening of our relationship with God, but that loss has been keenly felt ever since. I can empathize with her feelings as she sensed Jesus was "leaving" her. Her journal became more and more believable.

As I continued to read Nicole's account, what was so impressive was that Jesus did not solve Nicole's problems, but gently guided her to think in different directions until she gradually learned to see things differently,

or to view a problem or a situation from a different perspective which then helped her to make sense out of something that before was baffling. Another revealing characteristic of the conversations was how non-judgmental Jesus was in the way he dialogued with her. So often when she had misgivings about herself or something she was doing, Jesus would merely suggest options. The delicacy of this way of dealing with her struck me as being so fitting for God, who has no need to bungle into our lives, or to impulsively pressure us to do His bidding, or to clobber us when we make a mistake. That God should be so insecure! So many things in the book ring true and present a whole new facet of God.

The notes written down in *The Little Notebook* were written so randomly that it is obvious Nicole was not trying to make a statement or prove a point, but merely relating a series of actual experiences. What does come through in a very graphic way when you analyze the dialogues in depth is that Jesus was gradually and subtly reassuring her that the path she had embarked on, though new to her and unsettling to her sense of security, was the path He wanted her to follow, and she should not be afraid. He also gently and imperceptibly was putting together disjointed pieces of her life and her relationships in such a way that it was like pieces of a mosaic which when looked at individually have little meaning, but when viewed all together show a magnificent pattern, the way God so lovingly works in all of our lives. At times you get the strong sense that even the tortured and the troubled and the addicts she worked with have an important role to play in God's overall plan for His human family. No one is insignificant or superfluous. Everyone, no matter how lowly we may consider them or how useless they may appear to hearts

without faith, has a necessary role to play in the tapestry of God's masterpiece.

What I think is so important about the book is its revelation of a God who is so different from the God as so many view Him, not a God for Whom everything is black and white and rigidly ordered, but a God who shows such exquisite respect for His children and shows this respect in the way He accepts their use of the freedom He gave them even when decisions they make are not the way He would do things, and in the wonderfully sensitive way He suggests another course of action that might be more effective or better for us. God seems to be a master of options in His adjusting to the decisions we make, so that all things will ultimately work for our good. Only God could be so patient and so tolerant. Nicole might add here that God is always in the picture, and He acts if we ask Him.

So many extraordinary things are happening in the world today, and God's presence is manifested in so many graphic ways, one cannot help but feel that God sympathizes with our difficulty in finding Him in the confusing morass of our complex culture, so far removed from the original experience of the Resurrection, and is bending down to help us see the reality of His existence and His caring love for us in the darkness of our troubled times.

I hope this book finds the readership it deserves, because it has messages far deeper than the mere words that come across the pages. Though the book is so simply and so unassumingly written, this little notebook will touch the lives of its readers in a way that few other books will ever do. I hope someday I can meet Nicole. In her beautiful soul Jesus has chosen to express in a powerful way His love and caring for the tortured and

troubled who in their loneliness roam the streets of our highly cultured civilization unwanted and despised. What messages is God trying to beam to us through this disturbing phenomenon? These people do not wander around in our midst by accident. They are walking messages direct from God. I have a haunting feeling that God is trying to shake up our values. It is difficult for us to see value in the unproductive and the unwanted. One day we may be surprised to see street people and rejects in high places in heaven, while we ourselves from a more lowly place look upon them with admiration and honor. God's values are as far above ours as the stars are above the earth. Perhaps one day we will understand.

Translators' Introduction

Across the green fields of the Beauce, the rich wheat-growing region of France southwest of Paris, the famous silhouette of the cathedral of Notre Dame de Chartres has beckoned to pilgrims for eight hundred years. Americans are likely to identify Chartres with the cathedral. To the people who live there, however, the city is not only the site of that great medieval structure, but also a bustling regional center with typically modern economic and social problems, among them the needs of the poor.

Concern for the poor, particularly the homeless men who somehow survive on the fringes of society, led a woman of Chartres to help establish and become the first director of a home for such men in 1981. It was called the Compagnons du Partage, a phrase not very satisfactorily translated as "Companions in Sharing." She started on a shoestring, aided by Bernard Dandrel, who later founded the first European Food Bank, and the first year in particular was touch and go.

The woman's name was Nicole. She came from a distinguished family and was well educated. In fact, she held a degree in British literature and had taught for a time before her marriage to Philippe Gausseron. The two of them combined intelligence and style in a way one thinks of as characteristically French: understated, responsible, serious, but also attuned to warm friendship and the joy of living.

At the time Nicole started her home for homeless men she was in her late thirties, and she and Philippe had three children—Laurette, Benoît, Thierry—ages seven to eleven. She had recently had the charismatic experience of baptism in the Holy Spirit, and she had come to know the poor through volunteer service with Secours Catholique, a national charitable organization of the Catholic Church in France, of which Philippe was for ten years the local president.

Some of the poor, she discovered, needed not only a meal but a place to live and work, at least for a time. She set about providing such a place. The mayor of Chartres made available without rent an unused barracks on the edge of town. Friends and well-wishers contributed odds and ends of furniture. The first day the doors were open, three men moved in; the second day, seven more. The Compagnons du Partage was off to a shaky start, depending upon Nicole's constant attention to keep going.

The story of the Compagnons du Partage is more complicated than that, of course, but it is only incidentally the story of this book, which begins about four years after the founding of the Companions and transposes Nicole's experience to a universal and timeless level. Struggling to care for her two communities, as she calls them—her family and the men who came to live at the Companions—and always with inadequate resources, she was on the brink of abandoning her efforts after nine months of struggle when Pierre Maghin came to live with the Companions. Pierre was a priest of the archdiocese of Paris who, with his bishop's blessing, had become a worker priest in the late 1960s. Bernard Dandrel had met him at a charismatic prayer meeting in Chartres and approached him about becoming the di-

rector of the Community. On the day that he reserved the Sacrament in a makeshift chapel, Nicole knew that the Compagnons du Partage would continue. It was for her the beginning of a new relationship to Jesus. In the celebration of the Eucharist in this modest setting, Jesus revealed his presence as a living person with feelings of his own, a friend sharing her burdens and her joys, the Lord speaking to her and to others through her about their indispensable part in his kingdom.

This book is a record of that encounter, kept day by day in her *"petit cahier,"* her little notebook. In 1992, she allowed it to be privately printed in France and sold for the benefit of the Compagnons du Partage. In the American version, the journal format has been kept intact but divided into chapters. As far as possible, the informal, sometimes cryptic, sometimes inconsistent style of notebook entries has been preserved in the translation.

A few words about how to read the book may be helpful. It is first of all virtually devoid of the reverential tone that we are accustomed to in works of piety. The style is much more like that of the Gospel accounts of Jesus' ministry—episodic, terse, objective. Continuity results from the development of central themes rather than from sustained narrative. This method is incremental. It builds to something of great substance and consistency, but the reader can only know that—as Nicole came to know it—by starting with slight and fragmentary impressions.

Impressions is a key word. Nicole is not a visionary. In one of her first entries in the notebook, she observes that the Lord is "seated beside us" but that "It's not a shadow or an apparition but a presence." She often gives this

presence a visual form and a location but never a detailed description. The Lord is standing beside the altar, seated on the floor, clothed in a white mantle, accompanied by many people who contributed to Nicole's life experience: nothing more by way of description. Even the piercingly real impression of being present at the Last Supper is conveyed without any attempt to describe the scene. Moreover, as the journal progresses, visual impressions of Jesus' presence become fewer and fewer and finally disappear altogether. At the thematic high point of the book, the voice of God in the Algerian desert is presented without any sensory detail.

Readers may be curious to know whether the Lord's presence and voice were somehow evident to those around Nicole as her conversations with him took place. The answer is that they were not, that her experience was interior, as one gathers from a number of passages in her journal. Questioned by her son Benoît, she grants that she does not hear the Lord's voice exactly the way she hears ordinary conversation but that the voice is nevertheless distinct. On a number of occasions she repeats to others present what the Lord has just addressed to them through her. Commenting on the most surprising of her impressions, she says, "Interiorly I really am dancing with him."

If her experience was interior was it still in some way betrayed by the way she looked? Apparently not. She records only one remark that bears on her appearance. One afternoon as she gets into the truck to ride back to Chartres from the farm her driver observes that she has a faraway look. The Lord has just spoken with her about using one room at the farm as a chapel, and she agrees with her driver that yes, she is in a way somewhere else. This is as far as she goes in describing how others saw

her, and it is ordinary enough. In fact, the whole tenor of her book argues against sensationalizing her experience by dressing it in mystical phenomena.

The notebook offers neither visions nor special revelations. Quite the contrary, Nicole earns a firm rebuff whenever she pushes the boundary of divine omniscience. "Is there a hell?" she asks, and Jesus replies, "Why are you so concerned about my Father's affairs?" When she would like to know what will become of some unfortunate men, Jesus tells her, "Don't try to know everything." This steadfast refusal to traffic in inside information about the spiritual realm, to claim privileged insights or private revelations, is to our mind one of the strongest arguments for the authenticity of the notebook. The words of Jesus that Nicole reports tell us no more than the Gospels tell us.

The value of the book lies in its cogent reminder of how much the Gospels do tell us about Jesus—and about ourselves in relation to him. There is nothing imaginary or remote about the Jesus who speaks to Nicole, smiles at her, is amused by her recollection of a tag from an old love song, shows just a hint of weariness in reassuring her of his love for the umpteenth time, and once, to her astonishment, admits to a touch of jealousy. If the risk for believers is to relegate Jesus to resplendent glory as the Kyrios, the glorified Lord who is remote from daily life and correspondingly irrelevant, the Jesus who speaks in these pages insists on avoiding that risk by being one of us here and now.

The bedrock reality is that he lives now and seeks a personal relationship with those who believe in him. This assurance is repeated, emphasized. "I'm not an abstract idea or a system, but a living person." "[If you] file me in a drawer . . . I'll spill out of the drawer." "We are

two." He and Nicole play a duet, each needing the other to bring the score to life. Their relationship should become so intimate that she breathes with his breath—to which Nicole, in typically French fashion, responds, "*Oh la la!* I wonder if the Lord isn't going a little too far." The culmination of this imagery is his invitation to her, on a particularly hectic and care-fraught day, to dance with him. She is first incredulous, then scandalized. He persists, and in the end she says, "I let myself be led by him, and I'm happy, profoundly happy."

Augustine could not have put it more succinctly: the joy of unity in divine love. But Nicole is refreshingly unstudied and unpedantic. Even her description of the believer's participation in the life of the Trinity, at the conclusion of chapter 8, comes across in the simplest of language, although it is theologically exact. A large part of the book, in fact, is the story of Nicole herself, or rather the world of her two communities. She herself points to the ordinariness of her life. While those who know her might think that she is anything but ordinary in her moral concern and her social commitment, the point is well taken. She does not fit stereotypes of the saintly. Far from being withdrawn from the world, she takes her children on holiday, does Christmas shopping with a song in her heart (!), goes on vacations from Algeria to Finland, and loves to spend a day in Paris with a friend. She at first fears that such pleasures are incompatible with full commitment to Jesus, but he assures her, "I am the one who gives [such moments] to you to enjoy."

In fact, he gives her her whole life and he loves her as she is. Does she nonetheless share in the cross? Unquestionably, both in her work with the Companions and in her compassion for friends and strangers who suffer illness, disaster, or death. Her repeated expres-

sion of concern for others occasions what is perhaps the
most surprising theme in the book, one that may jar
readers accustomed to easy pieties about serving God in
one another. Jesus teaches Nicole that she must first of
all respond directly to his love, attend to him, recognize
his priority. She is free, as all are, to respond to him or
not. He will not bind her; you do not bind those you
love, and besides, he and his Father "have no need for
puppets." But if she responds to his love, she must not
forget him in her concern for others. In the end she can
do nothing for others that he does not do through her,
and he is also in those others, even those drunks who
have no religion and who leave the Compagnons du
Partage to all appearances no better off than when they
came. Her responsibility and what she can do for others
are limited; her relationship to Jesus is unlimited.

This is a lesson that Nicole learns only gradually, but
she learns it well. Over and over she protests that she
needs to *do* something, and she complains that in spite
of the best efforts she and her colleagues put forth, the
results are trifling, virtually meaningless, in fact. But
Jesus' response is always the same: Who are you to judge
what is trifling and what is not? Don't think that you
have to change these men. The part you have to play is
to love them. I'll do what you can't do. Don't be afraid.

That last admonition is perhaps the most constant
word that Jesus speaks to Nicole. Again and again he
tells her: Don't be afraid. Don't worry. Don't fret. Finally,
at the end of her notebook, Nicole is able to say, "It
seems to me that all I have to do is let the current of this
little notebook flow out. It's natural and in a way so easy
and simple. . . . The difficulties of the moment aren't
taken away, but deep down within me there's a center of
peace. It's new and powerful."

Nicole continues to direct the Compagnons du Partage and to befriend the homeless and broken men who come to live and work together on the outskirts of Chartres. They, in turn, continue to reveal to her not only a Jesus who shares in the sufferings of this world, but a Jesus who loves her and all people with a love that is unconditional and boundless. In one of the most poignant passages in her notebook, Nicole describes the arrival at the Companions of Lulu and Chevalier, two of Chartres' well-known and colorful street people. Lulu resists Nicole's attempts to give her a bath but finally yields to the gentle persuasion of her companion, Chevalier. As he caresses Lulu and tells her how much he loves her, Nicole is given what she describes as a piece of eternity: the absolutely clear certitude that Jesus loves us unconditionally, in spite of our depravity and our failures.

One of the most important features of this remarkable journal is its implicit claim that a deeply personal and experiential knowledge of God goes hand in hand with deeply personal and experiential service to the poor. That claim is, of course, at the heart of the New Testament: "How does God's love abide in anyone who has the world's goods and sees a brother or sister in need and yet refuses help?" (1 John 3:17). It is not uncommon, however, to find Christians—today as well as in times past—dividing themselves into opposing camps: those who claim to be true disciples of Jesus because they devote themselves to the "spiritual" life, and those who claim to be his true followers because they work for "social justice." Nicole's experience of an intensely personal relationship with Jesus is grounded in her direct and loving contact with people who smell bad, who cheat, lie, and steal—even from her—and is thereby rendered all the more authentic.

Some readers familiar with the charismatic movement may find it surprising that the Holy Spirit is not
more prominently present in these pages. As Father
Marie Leblanc, O.S.B., writes in his introduction to the
original French version, however, "Even though the
Holy Spirit is not often mentioned by name, that Spirit
is subtly present in the love of the Lord Jesus who leads
her to the Father, which is precisely the pattern of salva-
tion spelled out for us by the Gospel."

Finally, a word should be said about the distinctly
"Catholic" tone of this journal. Many, perhaps even most,
of Nicole's dialogues with Jesus occur at mass, usually in
the chapel of the Companions where Pierre celebrates
daily, on other occasions at her parish church of Saint
Aignan, the Benedictine monastery of Saint-Benoît-sur-
Loire, the chapel of the Sisters of Bon Secours, or elsewhere. When Pierre is gone, Nicole often spends a half
hour in prayer before the Blessed Sacrament, the consecrated bread, which, according to Catholic belief, continues the real presence of Jesus Christ.

Belief in the real presence of Jesus in the sacrament
of the Eucharist and the act of remaining before it in an
attitude of adoration provide Nicole with a way of fo-
cusing her attention and prayer. But it should also be
noted that Nicole's practice of gazing at the consecrated
bread is more than just a method or technique for entering into a more contemplative style of prayer. What it
offers is a way of prolonging the act of praise and
thanksgiving that is central to eucharistic worship and
to the Christian life. Often she complains that it is hard
to turn to praise in the midst of so much suffering. Patiently and lovingly, Jesus shows her that praise and
thanksgiving are not ultimately to be located in feelings
of well-being, or in understanding why things are as

they are, but in maintaining a heart-to-heart relationship with him in spite of and in the midst of suffering.

Nicole's sense of the immediate presence of Jesus during the eucharistic celebration is rooted in and shaped by the Scriptures. Since the liturgical reforms of the Second Vatican Council (1962–65), the first part of the mass, the "Liturgy of the Word," makes provision for a semicontinuous reading of the books of the Bible. On numerous occasions the dialogue between Nicole and Jesus is directly related to the scriptural passages that are read and meditated on in the celebration of the Eucharist. As one might guess from reading her notebook, the style of the celebration of the Eucharist in the chapel of the Companions is quite different from the "oh-so-traditional" Sunday liturgies in her parish church. At the Companions the pace is more relaxed, and there is ample opportunity for personal and spontaneous prayer. Nicole's words to Jesus are sometimes spoken aloud during these pauses for personal prayer, and on occasion Jesus asks her to convey his words to the small congregation that has come together for worship. In this translation, where statements of Jesus are addressed through Nicole to others, "you" has been qualified in various ways to make the meaning clear.

It may be helpful to note that the men who seek shelter at the Compagnons du Partage are welcomed in the name of Jesus, but are not obliged to participate in any religious activities. The only conditions for living in the Community are that they not use drugs or alcohol and that they be willing to contribute to the work of the Community during their stay, which for most is a period of about three months. The work consists of col-

lecting and repairing used goods and selling them in a secondhand store.

The Hermitage to which Nicole often refers is a farm about five miles from Chartres acquired in 1985 to provide more adequate living quarters for the Companions. The administrative center and place of work on the outskirts of the city is consistently referred to as the Community, and "Companion" is capitalized when it refers to a resident of the Compagnons du Partage. The names of persons other than Nicole's family, Pierre Maghin, Bernard Dandrel, and some close friends have been altered to preserve anonymity.

In our judgment this is a remarkable book that modestly makes an extraordinary claim: that the Jesus of faith has given this teaching about himself to a woman of Chartres in our time. We have found that this "little notebook" of Nicole Gausseron reveals its depths only on repeated reading. It needs to be read straight through in order to gain a sense of the movement of the journey on which Jesus asks his followers to embark, but it is also a book that rewards the random reader. On almost every page is a word or statement that helps one understand more clearly and concretely that a deep, personal relationship with Jesus—and through Jesus, with God—is the heart and soul of the Christian life, and that it contributes to the "weaving of the kingdom," as the little notebook would put it, when it is given expression in a preferential love for the poor.

William Skudlarek, o.s.b.
Hilary Thimmesh, o.s.b.

Saint John's Abbey
Collegeville, Minnesota

1

0

You Belong to Me

March 22, 1985

The Beauce isn't really flat. That's what I'm thinking about on my way to see my friend Cécile, who has just lost her husband, fifty-four, to lung cancer. It was only last night that the three of us spent an hour and a half together at the hospital.

Cécile asked me to pray for him. The only words that came to my lips were "Mary . . . Mary . . . Jesus . . . Jesus . . . ," and then all by myself I labored through the Our Father and the Hail Mary. Silently I begged, "Lord, take him soon. Come for him. He's ready. Take him." In my anguish I cried out, "Hurry up, Lord! What are you waiting for?"

Yes, I dared to ask him what he was waiting for! And now in the car driving back to see Cécile again, I dare to speak to him:

–Lord, what am I going to say? How can I console her?

–Don't search for words, Nicole. Don't prepare anything.

–Lord, it's hard for her. It's terrible.

–Yes, I know, Nicole, I know.

The road runs on. Silence sets in. The sight of the snow on the fields is lovely and soothing. I start to cry.

–Nicole, why do you blame me? You're asking me to render an account. Nicole, Nicole . . .

–Lord, it's hard to follow you. I don't know where I'm going.

I weep. My tears flow abundantly. There are only the two of us so I don't care. I'm not ashamed of crying. This is my way of speaking to him, too.

–Nicole, look at the road off in the distance.

–I'm looking, Lord.

–Can you make it out?

–No.

–And now?

–Yes, Lord, now I can see it.

(Didn't I just say that the Beauce isn't really flat!)

–Nicole, just now you didn't see it and yet it was there. Don't worry about your road.

–But, Lord, I'm frightened when I don't know where I'm going. I like to see the road ahead of me. I need to see it.

–Nicole, have I ever abandoned you? Mention once. Give me an example.

–I don't have any examples for you. I'm thinking, but there aren't any.

–Well then?

That's where we stopped. I didn't cry anymore. I felt his sorrow, not mine.

When I saw my friend and her five children, I didn't

bother trying to come up with anything. We talked and prepared the intentions for mass. During lunch we listened to each other. It was simple, warm, moving. You were there, Lord.

Now and then I am seized by a sense of vertigo. It will soon be four years that I have been involved with a community of twenty men. That's where my energies are spent. Physically, morally, psychologically, the Companions are my second family. If you want to help the "down and out," you have to go beyond words and pious sentiments. There can be no limits on your love. You have to let listening, patience, sensitivity take over your life. It's a road without end. You muddle through with what you've got at hand, with how things look today, and with what your own heart tells you. It's all-absorbing and emotionally draining even if I'm not at it twenty-four hours a day.

Yes, a kind of vertigo comes over me every so often. A little voice says, "What's the use? Why go through so much trouble for a handful of men?" Or again, "Ten years of study to become a teacher. You were good at teaching. Why put yourself out for a few good-for-nothings?"

This little voice full of reason and good sense leaves me confused. And then the other day on my way to the Community, the answer came, plain and simple. It was the image of a worn garment, threadbare, coming apart at the seams. This garment is the Companion who comes knocking at our door. The Lord needs us to patch up this garment with what we've got at hand, not to make a new one. We are responsible only for the sewing, the mending we try to do. If the garment tears apart anyway, it's not the fault of the Companions or of me personally.

March 27

Often during the Eucharist and especially after the Consecration, I have an almost physical sense of the presence of Christ. Standing or seated, his hands often extended, he invades me with his presence. I'm overwhelmed by a feeling of tenderness and simplicity.

I feel myself so protected at those moments that a strange numbness comes over me. I lose all sense of space and time. The people next to me are far away and yet very close. The experience is measureless and yet very simple. I shed tears of joy as I speak to him.

–Lord, I'm a little scared. Am I losing my mind? Why are you giving me all this? If it is you, you're pampering me too much.

–*I have chosen you because I love you.*

–Lord, why me? Look at me. I'm not worthy. You know very well that I don't put you in first place all the time.

–*Because I need you, Nicole, just as you are.*

The tone of his response seems to betray a certain weariness, as if he were repeating the same words for the nth time. To him it seems so obvious and simple. I discover at that instant, or rather I realize again, that I am a "sinner," but not in a negative sense. Rather, it's a lack of something, a lack of giving or of receiving. Experiencing the tenderness of Jesus immerses you. . . . You want to give back, to respond with thanks for this gift, and you realize how poor you are.

March (the chapel of the Companions)

On several occasions now, the Lord has been seated beside us. After the Consecration he's here. It's not a shadow or an apparition but a presence. Once at the

chapel of the Carmelite nuns here in Chartres, several times at the chapel of the Companions: he's here, seated, silent.

–Why are you sitting here, Lord? You're silent. You're not saying anything.

–*I'm here.*

–You must have something to say to us, to tell me. It's a bit disconcerting to have you so close. You put me at ease; I feel a certain serenity to know you're here, but I don't understand what you're trying to tell me.

No answer. Silence filled with his presence. Pierre prays in tongues. The answer springs to my lips.

–*Nourish yourselves with my Eucharist.*

–In other words, Lord, you simply want me to take advantage of you?

–*Yes.*

–But that's so simple, Lord; it's almost easy.

–*Yes, it is.*

His presence fills me. Once more I lose all sense of space and time. Around me it's as if everything were stretching away. At one and the same time I'm firmly seated on my shabby little stool and somewhere else . . . at one with him. It's nothing sensational. I feel perfectly calm.

–Lord, you don't say much; you're not much of a talker.

–*No, I'm not.*

–Pardon me for being so insistent, Lord, but I'd like to get this into my head.

Silence again. I have the impression of butting up against him, and his silence intrigues me. For my part I try to empty myself, to be completely new so as to get a better grasp of what his presence says to us. Gradually the meaning dawns on me.

–Lord, you are what for us is inaccessible, foolish, impossible. Is that it?

–*Yes.*

–Everything comes together in you, Lord. It's useless to look elsewhere. Is that it, Lord?

–*Yes.*

April 13

I have the impression that we have to strip ourselves of our customary attitudes, to be completely new.

April 19

The Lord is once more seated beside me. A silent and comforting presence.

–Lord, you immerse us in your love. It's too much, almost too beautiful.

–*It's free, Nicole. . . . It's easy. I've already told you that. Be like a wisp of straw; let go.*

–Why, Lord? Do you want to reassure me in the face of trials to come? Do you want to help me ahead of time?

–*No, it's free.*

–As if you wish to reassure me about what might happen.

–*I take the lead.*

April 22 (the Hermitage, our future home)

An old pig barn. The Companions have just cleaned it up. It's simple, empty, but still a little grimy. We were thinking about making it into a chapel.

Today I ask him:

–Lord, do you want it to be a chapel?

–*Yes.*

–It's quite empty and bare.

–*It's like me, Nicole.*

–Then we'll do it, Lord.

I had gone there weighed down by the events of the day, but suddenly I felt restored. As I get into the truck that takes us back to Chartres, one of the Companions says to me:

–There's something funny about the way you look. You seem to be somewhere else.

–Yes, Jean-Yves, I am kind of somewhere else.

After the Eucharist this evening the tenderness of God enfolds me. I'd like to stretch out on the rug, I feel so relaxed. My body is almost asleep, but not my soul.

I question him:

–Lord, you see our day. The people we've dealt with. It's heavy going.

–*Yes.*

–Following you is rather heavy going. You charge a pretty high price. We continually have to listen, be patient, urge one, comfort another. . . .

–*No, Nicole, I am not expensive. I'm always here. Come. Come and visit me. Take me. You can do that anytime.*

–Okay, I understand, but it's not restful or reassuring.

–*I am not offering you a freeway. This is another kind of road. It climbs, it drops, it turns. . . .*

And then in the silence, as if he were a little ashamed to put the question to me for the nth time, he asks me once more with the modesty of those who truly love:

–*Do you want to follow me?*

April 23 (*after the Consecration, the chapel of the Companions*)

The Lord comes toward us. He is carrying a bundle in his arms. Maybe a child?

　　–What are you carrying, Lord?

　　–*You and the Companions.*

　　–Why are you doing that?

　　–*To help you when things are too hard.*

　　–Do you do this often?

　　–*Every time you need it. When the road is easier, when it gives you less trouble, I let you walk.*

April 25

I walk to the Community along this grim, colorless street. To me the long row of gray houses and that endless military building with its empty windows seem to have no soul.

My heart sinks as I pass a disreputable bar for the umpteenth time.

Male or female, young or old, it's a weird menagerie whose path I cross.

　　–Lord, take a look at your humanity. It's pretty sad.

Silence.

　　–Don't you feel like talking, Lord?

　　–*I didn't spend my whole life talking, you know.*

　　–True, Lord. Do you have something to say to me?

　　–*Yes. Be.*

　　– . . .

　　–*Live. Be. Be yourself. Draw life from me. Let me speak and live in you.*

And in the evening, in the chapel:

　　–Lord, you're very quiet.

–*Yes.*

–Why?

–*I've already spoken to you quite often.*

–And so?

–*Meditate on what I've said to you. Internalize it.*

April 26 (the chapel)

–*Give me the whole place.*

–Lord, I thought that's what we were doing. Don't you feel at ease?

–*I need room among you.*

–Do you find things a little cramped here?

–*My spirit goes everywhere, as it will, where it will. Let it be free. Give it plenty of room.*

April 30 (the chapel)

This evening, an image of a deep torrent of water, violent, laden with debris. A huge black rock juts out from the riverbank. Branches and twigs bump against it, lodge in its cracks, then whirl away again in the current.

May (in town)

I pass by a halfway house for men released from prison. Everything is clean, the lawns raked, the flower beds blooming, the rooms tidy. And yet I know that the men there find the place stifling. They prefer the Community, even though our barracks are really ugly, our courtyard littered with paper, everything so dull and gray.

–Lord, do you see these wretched people in their gilded prison?

–*Yes.*

–They need something more than tidy rooms and pretty walks. What they lack is love.

–Yes, I know.

–Lord, what needs to be done?

–Pray. Ask me.

May (the chapel)

After the Eucharist:

–Lord, yesterday you told us to ask. I ask you that your will be done, but send harvesters for the poor, Lord. Look how they cry out to you.

–And I, I ask you, Nicole: Do you believe I can do that?

–Yes. . . . Yes. . . . You can.

–Well then, if you really believe it, I'll do it. I need the faith of all of you. I need you to want it with your whole being, to really believe I can do it.

–Yes, Lord, we believe you can.

–Do you accept not knowing where you are, being confused by my paths, my way of doing things?

–Yes, Lord.

My "yes" is a little timid.

May 6 (the Community, the Companions' dining room)

–It's my birthday today, Lord. It doesn't look as if anybody has remembered.

Silence.

–I was hoping for a party. You know how important that is to me. But the thought hasn't even occurred to them. You'd think I wasn't one of them.

–No, you belong to me.

May 7 (the chapel)

–Lord, it's difficult to be like a child before you.

–They have not only disfigured my face and my body. They have also distorted my words.

–What do you mean, Lord?

–To be a child is to let me live in you. To permit me to dwell in you, to act in you. It's enough to say yes to me, and I will come and love in you.

May 8 (the chapel)

–Lord, tell me why so many people go right by you without recognizing you even though they're looking for you.

–They're looking for the wrong thing.

–The wrong thing?

–They want an answer, a formula. But I have nothing to offer but myself, and that means a way of life.

–What is this way of life?

–To live with me, day after day, hour after hour.

May 9 (the chapel)

–It's hard to pray to you. When I come before you, I feel scattered.

–I am the one who draws things together, who centers.

–I feel empty, not up to it.

–I love all of you as you are at this moment. My love accepts you as you are. My love is simple.

May 10 (the chapel)

The Gospel of Saint John: "I call you my friends."

–Lord, you change our status from servants to friends. Does that mean we can ask you for anything we want?

–*No.*

–Look at the world. See how bad things are.

–*You don't know how to look.*

May 12 (*a wedding mass, Versailles*)

Text of Saint Paul, 1 Corinthians 13:7: "Love bears all things . . . "

–Lord, this "all" bothers me. Surely you can see that people don't do what Saint Paul says. Even two people who love one another.

–*You haven't understood it at all.*

–Well then, explain it to me.

–*With me you can get to the "all." It's true, in many ways you fall short, but I supply what is missing. I make up for your deficiencies. I come to the rescue if you ask me.*

May 14 (*the chapel*)

–Lord, what a poor tortured king you make upon the cross.

–*Why "poor"?*

–?!!

–*My body, my blood, these are the symbols of my royalty. No one can take these from me. I have given them freely.*

May 16 (*the chapel*)

–*Don't weigh yourself down with useless burdens.*

–What burdens, Lord?

—Life, the destiny of others, yesterday, tomorrow.

—Then what are we to do?

—Live this moment. I am giving it to you. It's my gift. Don't let yourself be preoccupied with what may be in the future.

May 17 (the chapel)

—I call you my friends. You are tied to me by a string, a thin thread, almost invisible.

—Why not a rope, Lord?

—Because then you'd pay attention to the rope and not to me. And besides, you don't bind those you love.

May 18 (mass, Noirmoutier, on the Atlantic coast)

"Ask and you will receive so that your joy may be complete" (the Gospel of Saint John). This isn't a place I'm used to, this remote little chapel with its community of sisters in gray and red habits. I feel a twinge of pain in my heart at the beginning of mass because I'm afraid that the Lord will not speak to me.

He enters and remains standing at the back of the church.

—Lord, thank you for coming, for being here for us and with us.

Silence.

—Lord, aren't you going to come forward and take a seat near the altar? Why do you remain standing at the back of this tiny chapel?

—Look, the essential is in front of you, my body and my blood. That's the way it should be. No one can distort anything.

And then a few moments later:

–Don't be afraid. I won't abandon you.
–I need to feel you.
–Ask. Ask not to be afraid anymore.

May 19 (Noirmoutier)

The little gray and red sisters are all smiles as they welcome us. From the very beginning of mass a sort of communion is established among us. The Lord comes to take a seat near the altar. He's dressed in white and he smiles happily.

–Lord, are you taking your place up front today?
–Yes.
–But why is that?

No answer. I realize that he's there just the same-- seated, still, peaceful. I don't understand until after the reading of Saint John, chapter 17.

–Is it to show us your Father, to send us to him?
–Yes.

–Lord, here I am crying again. Do you know why?
–Yes.

–You speak to me in the same way you and the Father speak to each other. I'm overwhelmed.

–Yes.

–You use the same language. It's powerful even though it's wordless.

I don't ask him anything else. I try to be as prayerful as possible. At the moment of the Consecration, Lord, you stood up and you became one with Pierre, who was celebrating. You were two and one at the same time.

–May your will be done, Lord. Where you will, as you will.

2

0

My Omnipotence Needs Your Weakness

May 20, 1985 (the Companions)

A difficult morning after a few days away. I have to get the house in shape, do the wash, clean, answer the phone. It's two in the afternoon. *Ouf!* In the silence of the empty house, I can pull myself together a bit. *Zut!* The doorbell! Since I can't get any rest and the time for my nap is past, I talk to the Lord.

—Lord, praising, turning to praise, is difficult.

—*Yes, I know.*

—There are tragic faces, crazy situations, Lord. That eighteen-year-old who just committed suicide. One can't praise you or thank you for that. It would be nothing but an empty ritual.

—*Not at all, Nicole. You see, on the cross I saw my torturers. Believe me, I know what people can experience at such times.*

15

–Lord, you weren't praising God then, were you?

–*Yes, I was.*

–But that's hard to believe. You were full of anguish. Of that I'm sure.

–*Yes. But you see, Nicole, I spoke to my Father. I spoke to him. Do you understand? I spoke. Even at that moment nothing was broken between him and me. That too is what praise is. So the torturers are there, you understand, but they are not the only ones there.*

–You want us to act as you did?

–*Yes. Talk to me. Talk to me.*

–You help me understand, or rather you shed some light on my questions, and it's like a revelation. And now I'm crying, Lord. When I'm with you, I often cry, but in an odd way.

–*Never mind. It doesn't matter.*

May 21 (in town)

In the truck that takes us to the Hermitage, I have a little time to think.

–Lord, we haven't seen each other today.

–*No.*

–Soon?

–*Yes. Don't do everything at once.*

This evening, since Pierre is away, three of us share an improvised communion service.

–Lord, you're here.

–*Yes. Take advantage of my presence.*

–Why do you want to live in me? Why do you visit me? You are surely life in full measure, but why me? What do you like about me?

–*Your vibrant spirit.*

–That's not much. It seems to me there are finer gifts to give you.

–*I don't know anything about perfect gifts. They don't interest me. What I want is to live with you, with your vibrant spirit.*

–You want us to love each other, and others to see that we do, is that it, Lord?

–*Yes. What else would you want to do?*

May 22 (at home)

I'm in the kitchen preparing a meal. It's eight o'clock in the morning. There's news on the radio about an armed robbery. The robbers were captured. I think about one of our Companions who is on the run.

–Lord, what will become of them?

–*Why do you want to know?*

–Isn't it obvious? Out of concern for them – or at least for him. . . .

–*Do you want to be my equal?*

–No. . . .

–*Well then, don't try to know everything. For us to love one another, I need you not to know, not even to try to know.*

–?! . . . !

–*Because from the moment you let me come into your life to act together with you. . . .*

–In short, to use me. Say it!

–*No, not really. No. To be with you and in you. I draw you to myself while you draw others to me. Do you understand?*

–It's a kind of contagion?

–*Yes.*

May 23 (at home)

I wake up this morning and think about the day ahead. Lots of decisions to make without Pierre.

–Lord, may your will be done. You're going to help me but I don't know how.

–*Nicole, you realize that I am revealing myself to you more and more. I'm not going to do your job for you but with you. I'm going to let you play your part of our duet.*

–That won't be easy. There's the Companion I have to take to police headquarters at Versailles. Who knows what's going to happen there? And then there's Lucien who was drunk on my doorstep yesterday. . . .

–*You are where you belong. You'll manage. Play your part and do what you have to do.*

–And you, where will you be?

–*I'll be the light that enlightens you inwardly. Let me freely play my part, too. You know that in a duet sometimes one plays louder than the other, but we are always two. You accompany me, I accompany you.*

May 24

Morning, en route to police headquarters at Versailles.

–Lord, are you here?

–*Yes.*

–It looks as if you're letting me handle this.

–*Yes.*

–I feel as if I'm a boss, and a tough one at that, but that's the way it has to be.

–*Go ahead.*

–What are the two of us doing?

–*Clearing the way.*

Evening, the Eucharist with Pierre. The Lord sits down and faces us, happy to see us there, it seems.

–*Ouf,* Lord! It's good to be here and rest awhile.

He appears happy to be with us.

The host is in my hand – light, vulnerable, oh, how vulnerable!

–You're in this little bit of host – light, fragile. It's crazy.

–Notice how light I am in your hand, Nicole. I don't weigh anything.

–Why are you so light, Lord?

–So that you can carry me better, take me with you, keep me in a little corner of your heart. I'm handy; I don't take up any room. You, my people, can be heavy.

–Heavy, Lord?

–Carry your weight, your human heaviness; that's how I want you to be.

May 25 (Pentecost)

Mass at our parish church of Saint Aignan with Philippe and Benoît. As we are on the way there, I ask him:

–Are you going to be there?

I'm always a little apprehensive. What if he didn't come?

After the Consecration:

–Nicole, do you want me to serve as your defender, your protector?

–Yes.

–I need an unconditional yes. I'll protect you in all circumstances, but in my own way.

–Yes, Lord. Thank you.

–Don't worry. I'll leave you completely free, Nicole.

–And if I fail you, if sometimes I don't manage to believe, Lord?

–Oh, I'll wait, Nicole. I'll wait for you.

–Then we're both free, Lord. In fact, we're partners.

–Yes.

Lover is a hackneyed and loaded term, but he's "my lover." He knows that I hate to be under anybody's hand, to have anyone impose on me, and he gives me

room to be free. I have the impression that my soul (or my being) is free to move as it will and that I go to him freely.

May 28 (in town, at home)

Three days off: the Pentecost holidays, a full house. The garden is full of sunlight, silence too. The children will be arriving in a few minutes.

–Lord, are you here?

–*Yes.*

–It seems to me that it's been a few days since we've been together. I feel a little dull in your presence.

–*Nicole, I'd like to ask you something. Would you like to give me a present?*

–Yes.

–*Take time for me. Now and then you take time to call somebody, to listen to the voice of a friend. Give me a call now and then.*

–You want us to become gradually more intimate with each other?

–*Yes.*

I opened my Bible and my eyes fell on the very beginning of the Letter to the Ephesians.

–Lord, you have given me the Spirit for my inheritance. These words seem meant for me. I feel somehow predestined.

He smiles and remains silent.

–I'm going to try to taste your Word a little each day.

He continues to smile in silence.

May 29 (at home)

Just before dinner I went out to the far end of the garden to spend a few minutes with him. While I was mak-

ing the salad, the image of a skein of wool had occurred to me several times.

–Is it from you, Lord? Is there something you want to explain to me?

Silence.

–I promised to spend some time with you, so I'll continue reading.

Ephesians 1:15–23.

–Is the skein of wool really you, Lord?

–*Yes.*

–You're at one end and I'm at the other?

–*Yes. Where do you want me to be if not tied to you, to all of you? I'm the one who untangles things, who pulls the thread gently, who avoids getting it all knotted up.*

May 30 (the Benedictine abbey of Saint-Benoît-sur-Loire)

Ephesians 2:3.

It's a beautiful day to be on the road.

–I'm enjoying life today, Lord. I feel in harmony with myself and with the world. Today I'm not letting go of you.

The images of a piece of knitting and then of a tapestry come to me.

–We often do let go of you, Lord. The stitches drop and unravel back to the start of the knitting. What do you do then?

–*I try to grasp my part of the knitting firmly but gently so that it will still hold together.*

–But, Lord, you're all-powerful. Why not have someone else take up the knitting where the stitch dropped? Look for somebody else to do it.

–*You miss the point completely. I wait, I'm patient, I handle my knitting gently. My omnipotence needs you,*

needs your weaknesses. I can't knit or weave anything by myself.

In the basilica at Saint-Benoît the Lord is seated at the foot of the altar, his hands open, surrounded by the fifteen priests who concelebrate.

June (on the road to the Community, in town)

–I'm not always reasonable with you, Lord.

–I don't like what's reasonable. I like things that are unreasonable.

–What do you mean?

No answer. I think I hear, *"Later."*

A few minutes later there I am in the middle of our secondhand store. One of the Companions, Alain, is drunk, reeling on his feet and teary-eyed. He lurches toward me: "Nicole, I have to talk to you." He weeps, he cries, he laughs, he shudders. There are a lot of people around us. Somehow or other we manage to make our way to the office. Alain is in a pitiful state. He weeps and clenches his fists, tells me about his wife, offers me some flowers he's carrying. I'm more and more distraught and sorry for him. He's a real case, Alain! His yelling shatters the quiet.

–Alain, do you want to pray with me?

–Yes, I do. I just went to the chapel for the first time.

–Listen, Alain. I'm going to pray with you.

–No! he yells. I'll start, not you! Lord, I'm ashamed of myself! You're my only pal! Forgive me. I'm ashamed of myself! Help me, Lord!

We conclude by saying a Hail Mary and an Our Father together. Alain cries and bows his head under the weight of his shame. I put my hand on the back of his

neck that is so weighed down and say this silent prayer:

–Lord, look at this child. He's yours. I give him to you. You can help him if you will.

Humanly speaking, there was nothing I could do. Alain fell back into his raving and took off.

As I was retracing my steps on the road I had just come, the Lord said to me:

–You have just done something unreasonable: you have put your faith in me. Yes, Nicole, I am also with Alain and in him.

June 2 *(in town)*

Pierre is back. The Community is nearly full except for those who prefer their liberty – the liberty, that is, to get drunk, drown their sorrows, forget. Paulo has left; Alain hasn't come back. I have a toothache and a heavy heart. The fatigue of a weekend swollen to bursting weighs on my shoulders and on my heart, too.

The image of a stream – or rather a sea of blood that inundates us – rises gently. I don't ask for anything. After the Consecration we talk to each other.

–Lord, this bath of blood. . . . Is it the one that washes us?

–Yes.

–You know, when I finish my bath I feel relaxed physically and psychologically. Is this the same?

–No, it's different. I wash you of everything that isn't essential. My blood washes away everything that you don't need to be concerned about.

–Do you mean Alain, Paulo, all that human suffering?

–Yes. I relieve you of your burdens. I make your task simpler.

–Thank you.

On my way back I felt lighter.

June 3 (the chapel of the Companions)

We've been going at top speed, buffeted by a thousand different things to get done.

The weather is hot and stormy, but it's good to be with the Lord. Just before the Consecration the Lord enters. He stands before us clothed in white. The whiteness is radiant.

–Lord, today you're standing. You're radiant. Dressed in your white mantle you dominate us. Why are you like that today?

–*So that you sense my presence. Just now I was in your hand and also at your side.*

–Don't you have something to say?

–*When I was with my friends I was seated with them just like this, and I said nothing.*

June 4 (the chapel)

Today he's here, but there are many people, an escort, around him.

–You're not alone, Lord.

–*No.*

I wait. After Communion the dialogue is more intimate.

–Who are those people?

–*Those who have helped you, supported you. Those who have led you to me. Do you believe that they're with me?*

–Y . . . y . . . yes. Lord, why are you telling us this tonight?

–*To make you grow, so that you realize that you're being helped and supported.*

It was as if the Lord were trying to tell us that he and his friends are the world of the living.

June 5 (the chapel)

This evening the Lord is neither standing nor sitting. We are united. It's good to pause with him.

—Where are you, Lord?

—*In you, in Pierre. I'm at home in you.*

I wait. At the moment Pierre raises the host, the image of Christ's face from the Holy Shroud appears on the host.

—Lord, is what I'm seeing really true? I feel very calm but I can hardly believe what I'm seeing, nor do I dare say it.

—*Dare.*

I tell it to the others.

—Why are you giving me all this, Lord?

—*To make all of you free of care so that you care only for me.*

June 6 (the chapel)

The Lord comes to sit down between Pierre and me.

—Aren't you going to say something, Lord?

Later:

—Don't you have anything to tell us?

—*It's good to be with you.*

June 7 (the chapel)

You came to take your seat in front of the three of us. You were smiling. I asked,

—Why are you smiling, Lord?

—*I'm happy to be with you.*

–But why the smile?

–A smile is as good as a wealth of words. Smile, all of you.

June 9 (the Carmel)

–You didn't come yesterday, Lord. You're here today. Where are you?

I sense that he's to my right, on the big crucifix that dominates the chapel.

–What are you doing there? What are you trying to tell us?

–My arms are wide open to embrace all of you, and my heart, open and bleeding, goes out to every one of you.

–Thank you. Thank you. I have found you again.

After the Letter to the Hebrews 9:15, I feel just a little upset.

–Those who are called may receive the promised eternal inheritance.

–I feel called, Lord. It seems to me I've already received my share of eternity. What do you want me to do with this gift?

–Nothing. Don't do anything. Let me live in you.

June 10 (in town)

On my way to the dentist this morning, I talked to him as I walked along, maybe to put the ordeal out of my mind.

–Do you want some space to live in us, live in me?

–Yes.

I feel in my entire being that his will consists entirely in this. This evening at mass I sense his presence. It penetrates me so fully that I feel it like a weight on

the back of my neck. I become quite limp, but it's a blessed tiredness. I seem to be almost in a state of weightlessness but simultaneously fully alert to what's going on around me despite my numbness.

I have the impression that the Lord is telling us:

—*Make an empty space in yourself, so that I can come in. So that you can adore me.*

I'm a spoiled child.

I wait for the moment after the Consecration – a blessed time for me – to ask him:

—Why are you standing dressed all in white, Lord?

—*My cloak protects you. I have already enfolded all of you in it. You are protected. You are already mine.*

Stupidly I ask:

—What do I have to do, Lord?

—*Nothing, Nicole. Let me care for you, enfold you, all of you.*

June 12 (Paris)

An outing. It feels so good to stroll without having to worry about time. Lunch with Chantal at a bistro. The tables are squeezed together, and you meet people's eyes momentarily.

—I enjoy life, Lord. But I'm still afraid that if I approach you, if I pray to you, you'll take away the things that give me joy and pleasure, like getting together with my friends. . . .

—*No, you're mistaken. I prolong these human moments. I am in them because I am the one who gives them to you to enjoy.*

—Then you really are the fullness of life.

—*Yes. You know that.*

June 13 (the chapel)

Before the Consecration.

–Where are you? I don't see you.

Silence.

–You aren't standing nor are you sitting beside us.

–*No. I am where you need me.*

–Where?

–*Resting on your wounds. Let me stay there. Don't move. Let me be there, in silence.*

It's as if he didn't want us to ask him any questions. As if, undisturbed, he could rest on our wounds and heal them.

June 14 (the chapel)

There's a tension in the air today. I feel it in myself and in the Community, too.

The Lord comes to sit down at our feet.

–You, so great, why at our feet?

–*To be at the level of your hearts with my hands open. To be within your reach. Let me enter. Don't do anything. It's so simple. I'm here.*

June 15 (the chapel)

There are three of us at mass today. During the day we had already spoken to each other.

–*There are some rough spots along the way. Don't pay any attention to them.*

–That's not easy, Lord.

–*There's nothing to worry about.*

And this evening the Lord once again wraps us in his mantle.

–This mantle?

–To protect all of you. You are bruised and bleeding this evening. You need my tenderness. Let my presence come into you. Taste it right now, at this very moment.

–Why are you showing me this?

–So that you may let yourselves be overcome by my love.

–Lord, my Lord.

I'm just babbling, but I have the impression of melting before him.

–I know why you're telling us this tonight. Deep down what I wanted was for you to come and calm and console and heal all the anguish I sensed in the others, in my brothers. But you tell us that we've got it all wrong, that first we must accept you, must let you come into our hearts, and not worry about doing anything on our own. And then you'll come and act in us.

–My ways are not your ways.

June 15–16 (in town)

An upset, stormy weekend at home. My little family lives out its mini-dramas and it seems to me I have mistreated you, Lord. In the midst of these little family squalls that wear me down, I seem to have left you aside, and yet . . . you're here, I'm sure of it.

This morning at the oh-so-traditional Sunday mass at Saint Aignan, you were there in front of us, reenacting with the same signs the meal with your disciples. Once again you spoke to me. Your word reassured me. Since I didn't write anything down immediately, I don't recall exactly what you said. Not wanting to misrepresent either you or myself, I won't write anything on your behalf today.

June 17 (the chapel)

There are four of us around the table. The Lord is here. I feel his presence.

–Where are you?

–*On my knees, at the feet of each one of you.*

–What do you want to tell us?

–*I want you to look at me. I am looking at you.*

–Why are you looking at us?

–*So that you'll look at me. So that we can look at one another.*

A little later, after Pierre has spoken in tongues:

–*Looking at my back isn't the way to follow me. Follow me by looking me in the face, eye to eye.*

It's as if he wanted to insist that we feel his presence and to tell us that he's alive, that love shines in his eyes, that he wants to live in mutual sharing with us.

June (at home)

I just had a phone call telling me that Marc, one of the Companions for whom we were able to find a job, has hanged himself. He had gone back to drinking. What a blow! I'm physically sick at heart, and while I'm washing my hair, I break into tears.

–We'll never succeed in rescuing them, Lord.

–*Look at me.*

–. . . .

–*Look at me. What do you read in my eyes?*

–Tenderness, as if you were saying, "I know."

–*Yes, Nicole, I do know. But it's you I want.*

–!! . . .

–*Turn away from Marc. Look at me.*

–It sounds as if you're trying to distract me, Lord.

Everything I have just written sounds crazy, and yet it's true. A little later on, in the afternoon, I'm walking to the Community and thinking how rich I am in the basic things of life: sunlight, good health, a positive outlook. It feels good to be alive at this moment.

–What is poverty, Lord? I'm so rich, and yet at this moment I believe I love you.

–*To be poor, Nicole, is to be rich in me. You and I among the rich, you and I among the poor, you and I everywhere you go, everywhere.*

This evening at the Eucharist, there are two of us and the Lord. I feel a harmony and an especially strong sense of communion this evening.

The Lord speaks to me:

–*I am in you. I live in you.*

And then my untiring question:

–What am I supposed to do, what are we supposed to do with you in us?

–*Let me speak in you.*

And later after Pierre speaks in tongues:

–*I will show you the force, the violence of my love.*

3

Love Leaves the
Other Free

June 19, 1985 (at home)

Between sweeping up and doing dishes, before Thierry's
baccalaureate exam in French and after serving lunch
twice this noon:

–*You know, Nicole, I'm a little like Philippe.*

–!! . . . Like Philippe?

–*Yes. He respects your freedom. He allows you to go out
to others.*

–And you, you're like him?

–*Yes.*

–Is that what your freedom is all about?

–*Yes.*

–Lord, you're absolutely baffling. You didn't say my
husband was like you. You said you were like him. I
find that absolutely astounding.

June 21 (in town)

On my way to the home of some friends. It's good to feel alive and on the go. Leaving the outskirts of the town behind, I emerge on the open plain. The shimmering stretches of green wheat fill me with joy. The streets I've just left behind are so ugly. On the side of the road there are poppies mixed in with what I think is wheat. I have the kind of heart that always melts at the sight of these little flowers.

–*Look at those poppies, Nicole.*

–They're beautiful, Lord. Such a strong red and yet so fragile.

–*The flowers are me, you know.*

–! . . . and the rest? All the green?

–*The human race.*

–What are you trying to tell me?

–*I'm like those poppies. Everybody sees me. I think they also love me. But it's so easy to pull me up and toss me out of the field.*

–You want me to let you stay in the fields?

June 22 (on the way to the Community)

On the way I walk by some gorgeous flowers. Then suddenly I have to duck to avoid a branch.

–*That's a sign of my kingdom.*

–What do you mean?

–*At one moment you're admiring the flowers and the next moment you're ducking to avoid a branch. Do this for my kingdom, too. Be supple and docile. Look up admiringly, but also bend over.*

Later on, after Communion, he makes himself clearer.

—Like Mary, be flexible and gentle when you speak to me and about me.

June 23 (out in the country)

A day with some friends. They have children in their late teens who are living in "concubinage." What an ugly word! We have lunch together. The meal is enjoyable but my heart aches. The parents seem to be happy but are still troubled by the situation. She's seventeen, he scarcely nineteen, and they're already sharing the same bed.

—Lord, my heart aches.

For better or worse, Philippe and I hesitantly try to say, "It's a little early. Don't go too fast." We do it as prudently and as gently as we can. A stroll takes us to a nearby monastery. The chapel of the Dominicans is beautiful and spare. A large figure of Christ on the cross welcomes us and towers over us.

—Lord, my heart is troubled.

—Yes, I know.

—Where are you?

—On the cross, Nicole. I'm not done carrying the cross. I know that it's for them that I'm here. I'm not done yet.

—Lord, tell me, what should I be doing?

—Nothing. Show me to others. Speak about me. Keep your eyes on me. Do what you've just done with them, with me. . . .

June 24 (the chapel)

The Eucharist. There are two of us with the Lord. I'm always a little afraid that he won't come to speak to me.

—Are you going to come?

–...

–Where are you?

–*Where I was yesterday, on the cross.*

–That must be hard.

–*Yes, terribly hard, but I hold on.*

–How do you hold on? You look like you're bending forward so much that it can't be by the nails.

His answer comes at the moment of the Consecration.

–*I hold on thanks to you and for you.*

I'm flooded with inner tears and also a few real ones.

–Lord, you turn things around. You need us, our adoration, here, at this moment. Your need is exact and urgent.

June 25 (the chapel)

The Lord is wrapped in the arms of his mother.

–What do you want to tell us?

–*When Mary carried me in her arms and when she gave me to other women, when she let others hold me, she was careful about the people she was giving me to. She wasn't careless. She didn't put me in just anybody's arms.*

–Do you want us to treat you just as carefully?

–*Yes.*

Later on, during the Consecration, the Lord is here – tall, living, all-powerful.

–Lord, I sense you are standing here – great, towering over me in a way. It's so different from the way you were just a few minutes ago – tiny and precious.

–*This is me, too. I am both. Tell the others that I am both.*

June 26 (the chapel, the Hermitage)

From the beginning of the mass Jesus comes to sit beside us on my right. A small voice tells me that maybe it's only an illusion, some sort of autosuggestion. I'm torn in two: should I listen to that small voice and pull back, or should I allow myself to savor this presence? I feel a touch of panic.

–Lord, I don't want to delude myself or you. Please reassure me that it's really you.

–*Don't be afraid of anything. Don't be afraid.*

–Why are you here?

–*To encourage all of you. To let you know that I am very close to you. I am a reaper like you. I'm here to reap the harvest with you.*

When we leave mass we learn that another Companion has hanged himself. I'm shocked, and yet inwardly calm. While Pierre takes care of the body of the man who gave in to despair, I go to break the news to the Companions. They're all sitting there, staring at me. These men rarely show any emotion, but when I tell them what has happened, they can't handle the terrible news and break down. I had asked the Lord to put his own words in my mouth. I don't know what the men heard, but I know that peace reigns in me and that it's the Lord who gives it to me.

June 28 (the Hermitage)

I continue to be at peace. This isn't the first time that I've been acquainted with people who have taken their life. But now I'm not stricken with grief, even though I share the sorrow.

We went to the Hermitage with Pierre to bless our new home. We pray. Jean-Yves, the Companion who discovered the body, listens to us attentively.

–I am entering this house. Follow me. Walk behind me. Don't be afraid of anything.

The house, our Community's future home, is blessed. I stop for a moment in the room that will be our new chapel.

–Lord, people are saying that we're off to a bad start. I don't feel that way.

–No, you're not starting out badly, but you are starting out poor. You share the poverty of the human condition.

This evening at the Eucharist:

–Lord, you want us to be docile and obedient. You want us to be like a pawn in your hand.

–No, not like a pawn. You don't understand.

–???

–You follow me, all of you follow me, and you obey me, but I won't "abuse" you. I'm treating you gently. Don't be afraid.

–Yes, Lord. I certainly felt that you were close to us. You were protecting us.

At Communion there he is in my hand, so fragile.

–You see, Nicole, you don't abuse me either. You carry me gently in your hand. I do the same for you. Don't be afraid. I'm here. All of you, don't be afraid.

July 2 (in town)

René, the Companion who committed suicide at the Hermitage, had a wife and seven children. He had spent some time in a psychiatric hospital. Humanly speaking he was at an impasse, buried under a mountain of problems.

René is fine where he is. As for me, I'm at peace even though up to now I have always reacted to the trials of the Companions very emotionally. It's not that I'm not involved, but I am at peace.

The burial today was simple and straightforward. The Companions were there, subdued and in their Sunday best. The family, dazed by its tragedy, is closed in on itself and oblivious of anybody else. The coffin begins to be lowered. I feel like giving his wife a hug as a sign of God's love for her. I walk over to her. It seems to me that for a moment her eyes brighten. "Thank you," she murmurs. A current passed between us, but what I really wanted was that you should pass between us, Lord.

July 6 (the chapel)

Before going to another funeral the next morning, this time with officials, firemen, flowers and finery, I speak to him.

–We hold on by a thread. Life holds on only by a thread. A very fragile and tenuous thread is all we have to hold on to the Companions. It breaks or threatens to break all the time.

–*Yes. It's fragile and weak. The thread is very thin, Nicole. Accept it as such. I'm the one who lends it strength and only I can make it resistant.*

It's true that the bond that unites me to the Lord seems terribly fine, almost invisible, and yet I feel more closely bound to him today than if I were chained to him.

A walk along some fields

–*Look at my kingdom.*

It's a field of durum wheat, I think. The heads are gold and green, a hard green.

–Your kingdom? What do you mean?

–*Look.*

–What do you mean?

–*The field is my kingdom. The gold is my gentleness. The green is my strength.*

–Your gentleness, your strength?

–*Yes, the gentleness and the strength I put in you. You are the heads of grain. The field is my kingdom.*

Your word, or rather your image, fills me with joy but also leaves me perplexed.

July 7 (Saint-Veran)

Today Jesus explained it to me.

Vacation in a little village in the southern Alps. All of us happy to have a carefree week without schedules. With my feet in the stream and my eyes on the mountain, I thank the Lord for so much goodness, for everything.

–Your kingdom is really beautiful, Lord. Thank you.

–*Yes, my kingdom is beautiful.*

–Not all of it. Here and now, at this moment, yes.

–*No, all of it. Look at the stream.*

I look at it. The water runs down over rocks and stones. Here and there are pieces of deadwood.

–The water, the stream, is you?

–*Yes.*

–The wood, the rocks, the stones are us?

–*Yes.*

–There are some that aren't even moistened by you.

–*True. But nonetheless you can see that it's all beautiful.*

–Yes, Lord.

–This is my kingdom.

On the mountain I reflect on this image when I'm not thinking about how much my feet hurt or worrying about falling. The Lord tells us not to stop at any one rock or stone. Each one is part of the whole. It came as a response to the question that I ask him so often when I read in the papers about all the catastrophes with their suffering and death.

–It's an answer, Lord, but not an explanation.

–I don't explain.

–What do you do then?

–I speak. I suggest.

July 8 (Saint-Veran)

From the paths the mountain is lovely. Philippe and our friend Christiane are happy. So am I.

We resume our conversation.

–I'd like to have you explain things to me. As long as you're talking to me, why don't you explain things to me?

–I can't. It's my kingdom, our kingdom. If you under-stood it, it would become your domain.

What it comes down to is that the Lord needs our trust, our childlike trust. He needs us not to know in order to be able to work, act, live with us.

July 9 (Saint-Veran)

Mass at nine in the sacristy. There are only six of us – three tourists and three elderly women from the neighborhood. The priest celebrates mass as if he were in a cathedral jammed with people. His voice rings out loud and strong for his meager congregation. It's a little

out of scale and yet the mass is moving. The Lord, attentive as always, comes and wraps me in his presence. He understands, and I feel safe in his arms. The experience is tender and simple. I can only respond to him with tears that have no sadness in them.

–Why me? Why all this?

–*Because I have chosen you.*

Up to now there's been a certain way of speaking that exasperated me. The way nuns talked about Jesus – as if he were their lover – rubbed me the wrong way. It seemed to me that they were exaggerating. I always thought of the Song of Songs as reserved to a certain elite, but now I suspect that a complete relationship (I almost said a sexual relationship) with the Lord is possible. It's not only possible for a John of the Cross, but it's offered to the mother of a family, which is what I am, to a perfectly ordinary Christian woman like me. It's staggering!

We move on to another spot. It's just as beautiful. There's a rock very close by. The stream flows over it, boiling up and covering it completely in transparent water.

The Lord gives me a knowing glance.

–*The rock is you, Nicole.*

–The water running over it is you, Lord?

–*Yes, it is. What do you see?*

–I see myself clearly under the water. I see both of us, but to me it's the water that's fascinating.

The Lord adds:

–*Show me to others. Reveal me. Let yourself be immersed in me. Show me to others.*

As I cast my gaze over the stream, I notice other rocks. They're beautiful and nicely located where they are. I realize that I'm no better than the rock beside

me. I'm just wetter, more immersed. I'm different, not better.

July 10 (Le Roux, Le Queyras)

Walking through meadows full of flowers. The mountain has changed. The harmony that reigns between us, the beauty of the landscape, makes me want to praise and thank the Lord. I feel very human and happy to be alive on this earth.

–And you, Lord, where are you?

–*I'm here.*

–You know, I get the feeling that when I really throw myself into the present moment I forget the spiritual world. I have the impression that there are two worlds, the world of human beings and the one that belongs to you, even though I know that's not true. When I'm happy, as I am now, where are you?

–*I'm here, but I get out of the way a little.*

–You get out of the way?

–*Yes. You do the same with Laurette, Philippe, the boys. You stay in the background when they're with their friends or with others. I do the same.*

–Thank you, Lord. I can understand that. I had asked you for another way to say "I love you," but you never gave me one.

–*No.*

–You won't give me another way?

–*No.*

–Why not?

–*You don't need another way to say it.*

–?! . . .

–*Does Philippe say it?*

–No.

–See, you don't need it.

–What do you mean?

–If you say, "I love you" to someone, the risk is that you'll stop there. When you say "I love you," you need to add, "Now do what you want."

–?! . . .

–Love, you know, is a space. It's an ample space that leaves the other free. Free to develop, to go away, to draw close. The essential thing, Nicole, is to be linked with one another.

July 11 (Le Queyras)

While I'm walking in the woods the idea of a musical score comes back to me. We treasure the silence, the time, the space we have to ourselves. I want to ask him questions, but I'm always afraid that he won't answer me.

–You want me to play my part of our duet, but you know that I'm very vulnerable. I'm sensitive to the beauty of people and things, to misfortune, to suffering. I'm vulnerable, don't you see? And what about you?

–I am invincible.

–And I'm . . . vulnerable.

–Yes.

–Is that really the way it is?

–Yes.

–If I let you play your part, will you make me invincible, too?

–Yes, and you already know that.

A few moments later:

–Do you offer to play your part often?

–Yes.

–But people don't want you to?

–No; they don't even know what I'm offering them.

–That must hurt you. I feel bad when I see people being mistreated, especially if they're being physically abused. That sort of thing disgusts me. But I suppose you feel more suffering than disgust for those who mistreat others.

–*Yes, that's true. I feel bad, bad for them. If only they knew.*

–You feel that bad?

–*Yes, very bad.*

Later on:

–Tell me, Lord, you don't judge, do you?

–*I feel bad.*

I come back to the topic obstinately:

–If you don't judge, if you love to that extent, is there a hell, Lord?

–*Why are you so concerned about my Father's affairs?*

–?! . . .

July 12 (Le Queyras)

We set out at the crack of dawn. My head is swimming, my heart pounding. We climb. This kind of mountain sickness is hard to take; everything's fuzzy. I'd love to speak to the Lord, but I can't manage. I content myself with putting one foot in front of the other and hope that I can get to the summit. We make it. The mountain is rugged and barren. There are rocks everywhere. It amazes me to see some little flowers managing to survive on these arid heights. For the nth time I say to myself, "How beautiful!"

–*Yes, you're right. They are beautiful. Be like them.*

–What do you mean?

–*Be what you love in them.*

–!! They're simple and bright, Lord, like eyes you'd like to dive into.

—Be these little flowers among the rocks. Content your-
selves with being these little specks of light.

July 13 (Le Roux, Le Queyras)

It's good to live and let oneself live.

—The present moment is good, Lord.

—Grasp it. Live it to the full. I am in the present moment.
I am the present.

July 14 (Le Queyras–Aiguille)

We have to climb to get to mass. On the ascent I feel a
bit distracted. I tell him so.

—Zut! It doesn't look as if I care much about hurry-
ing off to you today.

No answer.

The mass begins. The church is full. The celebration
is simple and prayerful.

—Thank you for Christiane, for Philippe. Thank you
for this harmonious week.

At the moment of Consecration I feel myself invaded anew. I sense a weight on the back of my neck;
my eyes fall shut. My eyelids have a hard time opening
twice to see the bread and wine elevated above the altar.
It is not I who adore the Lord, but I am turned into
someone who adores and offers. I'm still myself, very
much alive, and fully aware of what is happening.

—My Lord and my God. . . . I'm beginning to discover you, Lord, even though I knew you before. I always went to church. But now everything is different.

—Yes. You didn't know me well. I was like clothing you
put on inside out.

—!! And now, Lord?

—You're wearing it right side out.
Amen.

July 15 *(the train station at Grenoble)*

I take leave of Philippe and Christiane at the station.
During the boring train ride, I recite the Our Father and
the Hail Mary.

—"Pray for us sinners.". . . It always sticks a little in
my throat when I say "sinners." I don't think of myself
as a sinner. Tell me, Lord, is it a lack of humility not to
think of myself as a sinner?

—No. Once again you misunderstand.

—If it's not a lack of humility, Lord, what is it? A lack
of what?

*—A lack of obedience to the freedom of my love. A lack of
flexibility in allowing yourself to grow through me.*

—Yes, I understand. "Sinners" isn't negative. It's an
invitation to grow, to let oneself grow in you.

A silly, childish question runs through my mind.

--Why "sinner," Lord? It would be so much simpler
for you if we weren't sinners.

—Nicole, my Father and I have no need for puppets.

July 16 *(Moustiers–Sainte-Marie)*

Nothing. No, not nothing. A lot. I have the impression
that I'm accompanied.

July 17

—Are you here, Lord?
—You know I am.
—What are you doing?
—I'm letting you live. Take advantage of it.

And it's true. In my friends' house, the sort of house one dreams about, surrounded by lavender and open space, I'm as happy as can be. I let myself be spoiled like a pampered only child in the fold of Annie's and Gabriel's hearts.

–This is good, Lord. Thanks to them, to you.

–*Take it. I am giving it to you for your enjoyment.*

July 18

Up at six-thirty. I study Baudelaire. Suddenly I hear bells on the nearby mountain. A flock of sheep comes down the road in the morning light. The shepherd is behind them, leaning on his staff. He lets the flock graze. The scene is biblical. I have the impression that the Lord says to me:

–*You see – all of you see – I let you go before me to live, to taste and to eat of life in the moments I give you.*

July 19 (Moustiers–Sainte-Marie)

A moment of silence far from talk and chatter.

–It's good, Lord, to walk along the path above this little village. Your Nature is beautiful. I benefit from it, you know.

–*It's good you do.*

–Are you giving me these full and blessed days to arm me and nourish me for tomorrow?

–*Nicole, I am not a schoolmaster.*

–What are you, then?

–*A revealer. I open your eyes and reveal things to you as you go along.*

The image of something thrown in the water and making bigger and bigger circles takes shape in my mind.

–Could I say that your way is to work in concentric circles?

–*Yes, it's a bit like that.*

–Tell me, Lord, could it be that those waves get bigger and bigger until they touch other shores? Is what you reveal to me meant for others, Lord? Will you tell me?

–*That will happen. Don't fret about it.*

–Will you let me know?

–*That will happen.*

July 20 (Moustiers–Sainte-Marie)

The sun beats down on me on the road to the village. I speak to him.

–The road I'm taking is a little like the one you set before me, Lord. The thing to do is to walk and we'll meet you at the end?

–*No.*

–Why not?

The image or rather the presence of the Lord makes itself felt. He stands in front of me, his arms open.

–You're not at the end of the road but in front of me here. Is that what you're trying to tell me?

–*Yes.*

–Are your arms open to carry me when the going is too hard?

–*Not only then. When you're getting along well, too. Free of charge.*

The Lord seems to smile and be a little amused at me. I stop at the little church of Moustiers. I pour out my thanks to him, my prayers for pardon, my intentions, in one big lump. It's standard prayer, nothing special. I come out of the church at peace. The peace is interior.

On the road back he asks me:

–Why do you want to pass me up? Why do you want to walk ahead of me?

–You're right, Lord. I'm anxious to show my little notebook to Gabriel and to some other people, and to tell them about my encounters with you.

–You're going too fast.

The refrain from an old love song comes to my lips:

"Keep it to yourself. Don't tell anyone that love has driven me mad. . . ."

Now the Lord is definitely amused.

–Am I encroaching on your space, Lord? Is this your part of the duet?

–Yes.

Sunday (mass at Moustiers)

An old priest celebrates mass. The church is full but we are not together. A moralizing, threatening sermon dwells on the evils of our age – above all, sex. It grates on me. In part, what he says is true, but it leaves me tense. To calm down a bit I let prayer rise in me even while I go on listening.

At the Consecration the Lord appears above the altar, his arms open to embrace the whole crowd.

–Lord, I would have loved to see a tiny bit of your mantle behind the words of the preacher.

–Nicole, that's his way of saying that I'm feeling bad.

–You're feeling bad?

–It's difficult. People are difficult.

This touches my heart.

–Lord, I sense how weighed down you are. I want to help you carry your burden. What should I do?

–Keep on being the little flowers of my kingdom.

4

0

Don't Complicate Things

July 23, 1985 *(return home)*

Back to the fold, to the Community. It's always hard for me to come back to these sad barracks where there are so many problems every day. Going from one planet to another is always tough, and the little voice that I now know so well chants, "What are you doing here, Nicole? You're wasting your time. They manage without you." It takes some effort for me to get on board the moving train again.

At the Eucharist I don't experience the usual joy of celebrating mass in this chapel that we love so much.

–I'm not calm and peaceful, Lord. You'll have to accept me as I am. It's rather hard, you know.

–*Don't be afraid.*

At the Consecration:

—I'm leading you along. I'm taking you with me. Don't be afraid.

—But I'd love to know where you're taking me. Is it nice there? Is the place you're taking us to beautiful?

—You don't need to know. That wouldn't serve any purpose.

July 23 (on the road to the Community)

—Lord, the Compagnons du Partage is a veritable theater. I'm gone for two weeks and there's a new cast and a new show.

—I'm lending you these men. Don't make plans.

July 24 (the chapel)

—Be like children. Let go.

—Lord, you keep on saying that all the time. It seems to me that we are letting go. When you say you're lending us the Companions, do you mean Pierre too?

—Yes, I'm lending them to you.

—Why don't you want us to make plans for them?

—Because I know what you need. I know what's right for them. If you make your own plans, you keep me from giving you and them presents.

July 25

On the way to the Community I talk to him.

—Thinking over everything you say to us, Lord, I have the impression that you want us to be as light as possible.

–*Yes.*

–You want us to hold on to nothing, to nobody?

–*That's right.*

–I have the impression that I'm like a sea that's always in motion. I feel a little seasick.

–*Why? Let the men come and go in this Community. I've already told you: like leaves in the wind. Anchor yourself in me. I am the fixed point, the solid ground. You won't feel this heartache any more.*

–When we get right down to it, then, you come first, Lord. In a certain way the Companions come second.

–*Yes.*

–So I'm going in the wrong direction when I'm concerned about them first of all?

–*Yes.*

Eucharist at the chapel.

–*Leave me free to act in you. Let me be completely free.*

–Are we hindering you or slowing you down, Lord?

–*No, not really, but you're not resting enough on me and in me.*

July 26 (the Community)

Mass. Three Companions are here and a woman who is a friend of the Community. The Lord is present from the start of the mass. He moves about and goes from one to the other.

–Why are you moving about this evening, Lord?

And then, all at once, I am gripped by doubt. What if I made this all up? What if it's autosuggestion? What if . . . what if . . . ? I know this ditty well. It leaves me in a state of distress. I try to quiet myself interiorly.

My heart grows warm. It pounds a little and I hear the Lord say:

—*Tell them what I'm telling you.*

—But what if it's only me, Lord?

—*Tell them.*

I relate our dialogue, even though I find the presence of the Companions intimidating. I dive in.

—Lord, you usually don't move around so much. Why are you so active this evening?

—*Because I am* movement.

—Do you think that we're not moving?

—*Don't mark time. Don't ask too many questions. Get going. Throw yourselves into it.*

—Ah!

—*You say that I am living. Well then, since I look after you, get going.*

July 27 (the chapel)

The Lord is present in the back of the chapel.

—You're behind us, Lord.

—*Yes, so you can feel me. I support you. I am here.*

July 28 (the chapel)

The Lord comes and sits next to me. On my right. As close and warm and living as Philippe on my left, or as the Companions. He's seated like us, nothing more. His presence warms me and fills me. My head becomes heavy. Once again I feel like dozing off.

When it comes time to eat the bread and drink the cup, he seems to draw apart.

—Tell me, where are you going?

—*I allow you to taste my body. I am* inexhaustible.

What Pierre just said is true: "I am inexhaustible." It's not in my head. It's not my imagination. It is he. I feel myself engulfed in his presence.

–*Plunge into me. Immerse yourself in my presence. Happy or unhappy, you're all bathed in my love. I am inexhaustible.*

July 29

Seven-thirty in the morning. A telephone call from Pierre. There's been a ruckus among the Companions. Five of them have broken the rules of the Community. What are we going to do? It's eight-thirty. We go to the chapel to ask him who leads us.

Prayer. Question.

–What should we do?

Answer: Letter to the Colossians 4:2–6.

–*Devote yourselves to prayer, keeping alert in it with thanksgiving. . . . Conduct yourselves wisely toward outsiders, making the most of the time. Let your speech always be gracious, seasoned with salt, so that you may know how you ought to answer everyone.*

–Thank you, Lord. I wanted to bawl them out, but we didn't do anything of the kind. All five have left, destination unknown. Some said good-bye, others nothing. Not a sign, not a word of thanks. "You mess up, you pay for it." That's all there is to it. There's nothing more to say. You get what you deserve.

I recall what the Lord said to us:

–*You patch, you mend.*

–But the garment belongs to you, Lord.

At the Eucharist this evening, his message extends the Gospel of the day.

–*Be simple and little.*

–Tell us more, Lord.

–*Live. Take things, deeds, people simply.*

–Why do you insist on this simplicity, Lord?

–*Because that makes the task easier for you. Don't complicate things. Be simple. I'll give the increase in due time. If you're small and simple I'll be able to act "big and tall" behind you, after you.*

July 30 (the chapel of the Companions)

Not very receptive tonight. I think more about my black skirt, which I like very much, than I do about placing myself before him in silence.

–Lord, here in front of you I feel a little frivolous. I'm having some trouble entering deeply into myself in order to come to meet you.

At the Consecration it's always the same thing. He's here, living, present, attentive.

–*Plunge into me. I am invincible. I have overcome everything at every moment, everything that is – the beautiful, the good, the ugly, the malicious, the violent. I am here, living.*

July 31

It's a lovely day. We have the plans for our new living quarters at the Hermitage. Pierre leaves to lie down. The Companions are at the farm, glad to be working. The Beauce is still golden and ripe in the sun. Everything in me is singing for the joy of being alive, for seeing the others serene and, if not happy, at least relaxed and more or less at peace.

I'm getting the house ready to welcome my Laurette, whom I haven't seen for a month, and my friend Martine

and her children. My heart is singing for joy, and then, as I'm out doing my shopping, I suddenly encounter the nasty, spiteful face of Jean-Yves. He has just turned on a friend and must feel belligerent – and guilty, too. It's the stroke of a knife in the midst of our harmony.

–*Nicole, love him.*

–Look here, Lord, that's rather hard to do. He turned on me too, remember?

–*Yes, I know. Don't be afraid. Pray for him. Love him.*

–Do you realize what you're asking of me?

–*Yes.*

–How do you want me to act?

–*I'll go with you. Don't be afraid. I'll help you. You'll see. Don't do anything except pray for him.*

August 1 (*on the road*)

–*I have overcome everything.*

–All, Lord? Look at the papers, listen to the radio. Everything that's going on, the crimes, the wars . . .

–*All. It's not enough to believe that I have overcome everything. You have to live out that belief, too.*

–How, Lord? Are you going to give me a tape recorder so I can play it when the going gets tough?

–*No, you have to live out your belief. Don't wait to confirm it. Live it ahead of time, not afterward.*

–Why? You know how hard it is to live it.

–*Ahead of time, so that I can intervene. So that you can let me go with you. To act and speak and live with you.*

Mass at the retreat house at Thieulin a little while later. At the Consecration it's as if Christ were here once again, years later. He's always the same. Time shrinks to the point where yesterday and today are one. I have the impression of seeing the Lord and being with him on

Holy Thursday. The Last Supper isn't reproduced. It lives anew. It is.

August 4 (Saint-Benoît-sur-Loire)

–*I will heap joys on you.*

–I believe you, Lord. But tell me, how are you going to accomplish it? You know very well that life, that the world is sometimes difficult. Explain it to me.

–*When you talk about your studies in Paris, about what you discovered, sometimes at the cost of great effort, you claim that you have accumulated a wealth that belongs to no one but you, that no one can steal from you. Am I right?*

–Yes, Lord, you're right.

–*Well, I am your treasure. I am in you. You know that. No one can take me from you.*

–But heap up joys? How are you going to do that?

–*Not I, Nicole. It's you who are going to accomplish that. On any occasion, at every moment, you can come looking for me and find me.*

–What will you do?

–*When you're happy I'll be happy with you. When you cry I'll cry with you.*

–And when it's very heavy going?

–*I'll carry you. I'll give you someone to help you.*

–You have chosen me, Lord. You seem to want to cover me in your light, to clothe me in your mantle, in yourself.

–*Yes, that's right.*

–To do what, Lord?

–*To shine out and to proclaim me.*

–You could have chosen a more gifted servant than I. I'm not particularly gentle or peaceful.

–*I'll teach you.*

—So all I have to do is follow you and let go.
—*Yes.*

August 5 (on the road to Thieulin)

—We are – I am – a little dichotomous. Two worlds, that of the human, that of the spiritual.
—*No, you're mistaken.*
—What do you mean?
—*I give you these two worlds to live in, and you must shuttle continuously between the two, binding them together. Certainly you can see that if you don't do this you can die. You have to keep going from one to the other.*
Later:
—*Now you can see that your idea about eternity was wrong.*
—! . . . ! . . .
—*You tell me that the thought of my eternity makes you feel faint.*
—Yes, that's true.
—*Why? My eternity is the day when you'll no longer have to shuttle. The two worlds will be only one.*

August 6 (mass at the Companions)

Martine, Henriette, two Companions.
—*I walk with you. I'm at your side. I help you.*
—Lord, you have so much to carry. You want us to give you our burdens, but your cross is already very heavy.
—*It's even heavier when you don't give me your burdens.*

August 7 (mass at the Companions)

The Lord is here, on his knees before each of us. His

face before me – without any distinguishing features but powerful and compelling – seems to pull me toward him. I'm inwardly at peace. I have the impression that I'm sinking or melting in him.

–The world is in such bad shape. The troubles and the sorrows of the Companions. . . . What a hard time we have understanding.

–*Pray for what you don't understand. I haven't given you the world so you can dominate it by your intelligence. I've given you a field to cultivate. The world that is so close to you – the Companions, Pierre, Philippe, your children, your little world. . . . For the rest, you don't understand, so pray.*

August 8 (mass at the Companions)

The Gospel of Matthew 9:18–26.

–This woman and her faith, Lord. . . . Isn't her faith a kind of magic? Is it as true today as yesterday that all we need is faith?

–*Yes.*

–For me, too?

–*Yes. Aren't you sure about that? When haven't I answered your prayers?*

I think about it and it's true: the Lord has always answered my prayers.

–Yes, Lord, it's true. I have a hard time saying it, but it's true. You answer our prayers when we ask with all our heart and when it's urgent.

–*Yes, Nicole, yes.*

–Lord, I'm not asking you for anything for Pierre today. I'm not asking you to cure him. I didn't do it for Françoise, remember?

–*Yes, I know.*

–What about Pierre, Lord?

—Don't fret. Don't fret about anything. You haven't asked for anything for him. That's all right. Wait. Don't fret about anything.

August 9 (the Companions)

—Be like children. Stay that way.
—Lord, why do you insist on this?
—Because if you left me free, as children do, I would be able to show you marvelous things and give you gifts.

Heaviness and sadness today. I'm not too sure where it comes from. I feel like showing my little notebook to a friend. Pierre tells me not to. I'm going to try to obey, but I don't feel like it. I have the impression that the two of us, the Lord and I, are having an argument. We're not getting along very well. I try to say prayers of praise. It grates.

During the day this mood slackens, and this evening at mass the Lord is seated beside us, his elbows on his knees, terribly present.

—Speak to them, Nicole.

I say that he's here, sitting with us to comfort us and to tell us that he's with us, that he's here not to look at us, but to act with us, in us. It's powerful.

—Lord, you're looking at me. What do you want?
—Do you want to follow me?
—Look and see, Lord. Am I doing anything else?
—You feel like resisting. Let go.

The image of a big pipe appears, with water flowing from it.

—Are you the pipe?
—Yes.
—And am I the water?
—Yes.

—Why?

—*Let go. Let me channel you. I am the one who directs the way the water flows. Be willing to let go. You'll see.*

How can I resist him when I sense such care and such respect at the same time? I haven't the least inclination to obey him, but I'm going to do it, for I can't refuse him. That wouldn't be right, and yet . . .

August 11 (Brittany, l'Aber W'rach)

A mini-vacation with Philippe and Laurette. On the beach. When we arrived the sky was gray and it was raining. Suddenly it's all swept away and the sea changes color constantly.

—*Be adaptable, like the surface you're looking at.*

— . . . ! . . .

—*It changes, it moves, it turns red, it sparkles. . . .*

—Yes, I see. So you want me to let go and be completely at your mercy?

—*Yes.*

That's all!

August 13 (Brittany)

A reading from the beginning of the First Letter of Saint John. I balk at 1:10: "If we say that we have not sinned, we make him a liar, and his word is not in us."

The next day the phrase becomes clear: "Those who have been born of God do not sin" (3:9).

—But, Lord, I'm still a bit confused.

—*In what you have just read you have the front and the back of the fabric.*

—The fabric is you. It's in your hands. And sometimes we see one side, and sometimes the other, is that it?

—*Yes.*

August 14 (Brittany)

First Letter of Saint John 3:22: "And we receive from him whatever we ask, because we obey his commandments and do what pleases him."

–This is difficult to understand and accept. I don't understand it very well.

–That's right, you don't.

–It's the "whatever" that bothers me. You don't grant everything, do you?

–I don't grant just anything.

–Who is going to tell us how to ask for what pleases you?

–The Holy Spirit. You know that.

–But wait a minute. If we are to ask for what pleases you, aren't we just playing a game of hide-and-seek?

–Not at all. Don't get upset. I'll help you understand.

August 15 (mass at a little church in Brittany)

The church is full. Three priests are concelebrating, and the overall effect is painful. It's more of a show than a celebration. I find it hard to take. I imagine momentarily how the space between the altar and the people could be filled with singing and dancing.

After Communion I receive the answer to yesterday's question.

–Requests are made within the context of a relationship between you and me, between me and all of you.

–!! . . . What does that mean?

–You don't ask Philippe or the children for any old thing at any old time. It is the same way with me. You didn't understand yesterday because you forgot what is essential: the relationship.

–That's true. Now I understand better. Thank you.

August 19 (the chapel of the Companions)

Jesus is in the chapel with Mary.

–Why are both of you here?

–So that you may pay attention to Mary.

–What do you mean?

–Do what she did. She always said yes.

August 20 (the chapel of the Companions)

Jesus and Mary. They hold hands, and the way they do it reveals the great love that unites them.

–Have you both come back again? What is it you want me to grasp?

–Be like her. Effective like her.

–Effective?

–Yes. Present, gentle, self-effacing, but still radiant. Be like her.

August 22 and 23

A difficult day. At the Hermitage the Companions haggle, criticize, attack.

I listen to them and am a bit astounded and shaken. I try to hand it all over to the Lord, but it's difficult.

I meet with them again the next day, and this time I do the talking and try to clarify things. Everything becomes calm as if by magic. Pierre, who is about ten miles away, is helping us with his prayers. In addition to yesterday's bad humor being gone, I was able to put some home truths across to them very firmly. We parted friends and in a good mood.

–Thank you, Lord. You helped me when I was all alone.

—*I hold you in my hand.*

—Thank you.

—*The Companions lead you to me, Nicole. What matters is not being loved by them, but loving me. They are the ones who lead you to me in this moment of heart-to-heart exchange. Let yourself be led by them along my paths.*

August 25 (the Hermitage: first mass in our new chapel)

A large gathering of all the staff and the Companions. Some of them have a very difficult time sharing the same living quarters.

Mass. Jesus is here. He's big, almost too big for this tiny chapel. He's standing and takes us all in with his gaze.

—*I'm here. I arrived here ahead of you. Don't be afraid. I'm here, and I'm first. Let me always be in the first place.*

After a fairly peaceful meal, one of the difficult Companions decides to leave. Our problems are taken care of, for the time being, at least.

August 26 (the chapel)

The Lord is here, opening wide his hands at the moment of the Our Father.

—Why are you doing that, Lord?

—*Because we have the same Father. Make your requests of my Father. I am with you.*

August 27 (the chapel)

I have a hard time being receptive to him. Our two boys have just gotten back from a two-month stay in the States.

After Communion I have the nerve to ask the Lord.

–Are we good guardians?

–*Yes.*

(He smiles)

–Is something lacking?

–*Yes. Really have the heart of a child. Ask the way children do. I will do wonderful things. Believe that I can.*

August 28 (the chapel)

–*Don't be afraid. It's not only my hands I stretch out toward you, but my arms as well. I walk with you. I meet you faithfully. Don't be afraid.*

August 29 (the Hermitage, the new chapel)

Philippe and the children are here. And three Companions. The consecrated host is on the table. All of us are standing around it.

–*I'm malleable, infinitely malleable.*

–I'm a little afraid to say this to the others.

–*Tell them.*

I say: "I'm malleable like the clay that is to be molded. I will fill what is empty, straighten out all that is rough and crooked in you. Let me simply draw close to your hearts. I am moldable."

September (the chapel)

The Lord is walking along a road. He bends over to take something in his arms.

–What are you carrying?

–*All of you. You need to be carried. You are the ones I especially care for. I hold you close to my heart.*

After Communion the Lord tells us:

—*I know what I'm doing.*

September (the chapel)

From the beginning of the mass it's as if I'm wrapped in a cloak. Even though it's thick, heavy, and full, it's light. It's as if I'm a part of him. He lacks nothing, and yet no one is excluded. Those I carry in my heart, the men and women for whom we pray, are all included. I have the deepest desire to let myself sink into this numbness. I try not to fall off my bench, but the back of my neck feels heavier and heavier. I think it's a gift from the Lord.

—You're beyond words. I can't describe you, but I feel you and I know you're present. Thank you. Do you have something special to say to us?

—*Yes. I clothe you with my garment. I make you invulnerable. Don't be afraid. I've already told you that. I've chosen you, I protect you, I'm leading you. Don't be afraid. I'm doing it.*

There's something infinitely sweet and yet very strong in this presence that envelopes me.

September 4 (the chapel)

His presence is so strong that I feel like dozing off right at the beginning of mass. I resist.

A deep and all-embracing peace spreads through me. I bless the Lord and thank him. After Communion, he invades me, invades all of us.

—*I embrace you. Just as you are, with your limitations and weaknesses. I don't want you to be anything else. I want you with me.*

September 6 (the chapel)

A force seems to descend on the host at the moment of the Consecration. It's hard to put into words. It's like a great weight, but still light and airy. Gradually it becomes one with the host. It's comforting.

–What are you trying to tell us, Lord?

–*Feel this force and believe. You know and believe that I am present at this moment. Believe in me, all of you. Believe in me, the Living One.*

It's so strong it's beyond words.

Sunday (in the country with friends)

A friend confides in me. The load she has to carry and endure is so heavy that my heart aches as I listen to her. We are at the limits of what is human, on the brink of madness. I listen and feel faint for her.

–*Nicole, believe that I am here.*

So I simply and silently made this act of faith. Silently. . . . Happy are those who can share their faith, their hope. I was embarrassed to do so, Lord, so I said nothing about the riches I receive from you. All I did was what you told me to do: "Believe."

In the darkness, bereft of any human solution, I believe. You know how to dwell in the silence, Lord, so if that is what you will, play your part. All I can do is keep silent and call on you.

September 13 (the chapel, a half hour of adoration)

I entrust the Companions to him.

–*Forget them.*

–Why, Lord?

—You have come to see me, to spend time with me. Forget them.

I have a hard time concentrating on him. That will come. I'm just beginning.

A little later:

—Do you want to be my servant?

—Yes.

—I will make you a queen, the queen of my kingdom.

—An invisible kingdom?

—Invisible and visible.

The peace that dwells in me is profound. I experienced it all evening. If a doctor friend of mine were to read what I have written, he would probably send me off to the psychiatric ward, but he would be mistaken. This peace really comes from the Lord.

5

o

Leave Me Some Room in Your Hearts

September 16, 1985 (the chapel, a half hour of adoration)

Henri, a Companion, is with me. In silence. It's a gift.

I entrust the Companions to the Lord, those who are present and those who are absent. Also Christiane and her difficulties at work.

  —*Don't worry,*
  Jesus tells me.
  She'll soon be free of them.

And then I look at the host in its golden lunette.

  —*Don't worry. I'll help you understand. I'll look through your eyes.*

  —Tell me what you mean, Lord.

  —*The host you see is encircled with gold. The gold is my gaze on humanity. I'll come to look at people along with you, to help you see them as I do. I don't belittle your intuition,*

71

your way of looking at things. It's just as true as the host you're looking at. I'll come and wrap it in mine.

Amen.

September 17 (adoration in the chapel)

There's a great calm or, rather, a repose. I'm drained and empty this evening, and in the chapel, kneeling next to Henri, I offer the Lord all those I carry.

The Lord comes to us with a smile and puts his arms around us. I fall into a kind of weightlessness. I feel neither my body nor my joined hands. I stammer. That's all I can do today. As I leave the chapel, peace. "Don't be afraid." The other day a priest friend of mine, Father Guédou, called to tell me about his close brush with death: "We make everything so complicated. The evil one puts on a lot of nice faces, but everything is so simple. When you're close to death, there's very little that matters."

September 18 (adoration in the chapel)

–Lord, here in your presence I feel scattered, a little diluted by all the people and things I'm involved with.

–A little, yes. I'm only lending you these people, these faces, these events. What I give you – have already given you – is myself.

September 19 (adoration)

One of the Companions, perhaps the best one, got plastered. I'm heartbroken and am starting to feel faint again. The Lord is here. He draws close to my face and smiles at me. Yesterday's words come back: *"I am lending them to you."*

September 20 (adoration)

–*I'll make your house grow. Don't be afraid. I'll do it.*
–Do you mean the Community, Lord?
–*Yes. I'll make it grow.*

September 21 (conversation while walking)

–Lord, we're told we're not supposed to judge. But we can't avoid judging. "Don't condemn" I can understand. But "Don't judge" doesn't make any sense to me at all.
–*I've given you your capacity to judge. Use it. Completely. Don't hesitate, but don't pigeonhole people by your judgment.*
–Please explain that more fully.
–*Because I'm in them, too, in my own way, even if you don't see it or even sense it at times. Don't limit what I can do, say, or accomplish in them. Do you understand?*

September 22 (mass at Saint Aignan)

A heavy and difficult day. Too many things to do. I feel so exhausted I begin to cry. The Lord smiles. He walks down the steps and comes to meet me.
–*Do you want to continue to be my little servant? I'll make you a queen.*
–Yes, I do.

September 28 (the chapel)

During my time of adoration he came and with a smile very gently took me in his arms. It was simple and comforting.
–*Carry on. Don't be afraid. I'll spoil you.*

Before we part, I ask him:

–Send out harvesters, Lord. There are not enough of us. We asked you for a driver and you gave us one. A solution for one of the Companion's problems, and you gave us that, too. Now I'm asking for harvesters. You realize that with Pierre gone for a few days I can hardly keep my head above water.

–*I'll take care of it, Nicole. Don't be afraid. I'll give you what you need.*

October 1 (adoration, the chapel)

This time I'm all by myself in this privileged place. He begins.

–*You see. You have nothing to be afraid of. You used to be afraid that this half hour of adoration would be too long. Now you know how quickly the time passes with me.*

–I beg your pardon, Lord. You're right. I find peace when I'm with you, and when you talk to me, you put me back together again. You give me an invisible solidity.

The Lord's smile is full of tenderness, with perhaps just a little touch of weariness.

–Is my head or my heart too impenetrable, Lord?

–*No, not really. But you're a bit negligent.*

–!! What do you mean?

–*You get colds – and now you've just come down with the flu – because you forget to put on a coat. You move from one place to another without giving any thought to what you're wearing.*

–You mean I'm forgetting to clothe myself with you?

–*Yes. I'm like a coat. Take the time to clothe yourself with it, to slip it on.*

–Why?

–*So that I can protect you, and also act in you and around you.*

October 2 (adoration)

After a half hour with Jesus in the chapel, I go back into the night, dead tired. The day was terribly full. At home, the doorbell rings. It's Jean-Yves, a former Companion, drunk, sneering. He yells at me. There is hatred in his voice, something diabolic about the way he looks at me. I try to keep calm, but my heart goes cold. When Philippe comes home he calmly gets him settled down. Jean-Yves lowers his head, excuses himself, and takes off.

The children were present. We talk about it at table. Laurette says:

–I know why he insulted Mommy. I get like that, too. When I'm ashamed of myself, I yell at her.

And Laurette's only eleven years old! We talk about the poor, God, religion.

Thierry, who's sixteen:

–What you're doing for the Companions is good, but it's useless.

–Useless?

–Yes, useless. And that's why you should keep on doing it.

Benoît adds:

–It's not Jean-Yves you're saving; you're saving yourself.

There's no chill in my heart any longer. Quite the contrary. They restored me to peace.

October 3 (mass at the chapel)

There are three of us. The Lord comes and sits down alongside us. He really is seated, just like us, but perhaps a little more composed.

–I feel you so incredibly present next to us, next to me, Lord.

–I'm here to pray to the Father with you and like you.

–You are at one and the same time incredibly real and light.

–Don't make any plans or projects. Let me do things and act for you. I'm the one who is leading this Community.

October 4 (mass at the chapel)

–Don't dream about the impossible. Do what is possible.

This word of the Lord touches a friend who came for mass and to whom Pierre, just a few moments earlier, had said almost the same thing.

October 5

At Essonne for a diocesan meeting of Secours Catholique.

Pierre and I were asked to come and speak about the Compagnons du Partage.

I'm delighted to have an audience again, and this time I'm not trying to get them to love the English language but Jesus. In a way it's easier. I have a general outline in my head that Philippe prepared for me so I wouldn't go running off in all directions, and with it I try to speak calmly and simply about our life with the Companions. It flows easily, and afterwards a lot of people come to ask me questions and, above all, to tell me that they sensed my faith in the God-man who inspires us.

A little voice tells me:

–I'll make you a queen. Just as I told you.

An older man who's a little intimidating comes up to thank me. He tells me he's taking away just one thought from the whole day. I ask him what it is. He rummages

through his papers and reads it. Someone had asked me what our success rate was over the past four years, and I had answered:

"If you want a number, put down that maybe we succeed in getting about ten percent of the men 're-arranged.' Whatever efficacy we have or results we have achieved belong to the invisible kingdom."

I feel proud and happy to have passed on the message. Not conceited, but proud to have been a good instrument, a good servant, that day.

I almost forgot. . . . Another gentleman came running up to me just as I was leaving and demanded to know where my husband was.

–He's not here.

–What a shame.

–Why do you say that?

–I would have loved to meet this man. He must be a saint.

A little dumbfounded I asked him:

–Why do you think that?

–Well, you must often have to spend six to eight hours a day with the Companions. But you tell us that your kids are fine. So your husband must be a saint.

Cherchez la femme? Not at all. *Cherchez le roi* – Look for the king. He will enter the kingdom before me!

October 13 (mass at the chapel)

Pierre concelebrates with Jean-Marc, the abbot of Tamié. The congregation is just me. There is a sense of harmony right from the start. The Lord is standing, smiling, rejoicing over this complicity in the act of giving praise.

–*Come. Ask. I am an inexhaustible treasure. Dig in, not just with your hands but up to your elbows.*

Pierre asks the Lord why so few of the Companions know him.

–*Don't worry about it. I am among them.*

October 15 (mass at the chapel)

Jean-Claude, Anne Marie, and two Companions.

We didn't close the circle. The Lord comes and takes the empty space, sitting down on the floor!

–Why are you sitting on the floor?

–*I am the bond. I come to unite. I place myself where there is room. Leave me some room in your hearts. I put myself where you need me, where there is division and pain. Make room for me.*

October 16 (in the car with Laurette)

We feel very close.

Laurette:

–Mom, I went to mass at the Carmel with Dad yesterday, and I realized how much I like to go with him. But I'm not sure whether I have any faith.

–Why do you say that?

–What if Jesus' friends, the apostles, were mistaken? What if Jesus never existed?

–But he did exist. Leave the door of your heart open to him. Then he'll be able to come in and live in your house.

–I know what you're talking about. You and Dad have a lot of influence on me. I go to mass because you go, but it's not the same for me.

–What do you mean?

–When you pray, I can see that you really believe he exists.

Mass at the Hermitage

I'm overcome by a profound drowsiness. I feel like lying down. I feel so peaceful. I have all I can do not to stretch out on the carpet.

–Thank you. Thank you.

–*This is the circle of my glory. Many have already entered into it. You're a part of it. Be happy and joyful.*

A little later I say to him:

–It's difficult to hoist others up to you. It's a heavy task.

–*Be like the yeast in the dough. Be little. Don't worry about whether or not the dough is rising.*

October 17 (mass at the chapel)

–*Don't be afraid. I'll lead you to the other shore. You're on the open sea. You can no longer see the shore you have left, nor can you see the one I am leading you toward.*

–We are on the open sea, Lord. Sometimes I get seasick.

–*Don't be afraid. I am at the helm of the boat.*

October 18 (adoration)

It's hard for me to forget mundane things. Silly and "worldly" ideas weigh me down. I tell him so.

–Lord, it's hard going today.

And later:

–What we do for the poor you give us, for the Companions, is make them a little less poor. But when we do that, you make us a little richer with yourself. Is that it?

–*Yes.*

October (mass at the chapel)

It's the anniversary of the death of my friend Françoise.

Jesus is here in front of us along with Françoise. Her head is slightly inclined. They're smiling.

I'm flabbergasted.

–Why are you doing this, Lord?

–*So that you may believe. Do you believe that she's really alive?*

–Yes.

My "yes" is a little timid.

–*Believe.*

Later he says to me:

–*Look at her. Remember. I answered your prayer.*

And it's true.

–Lord, at least we're on the right road. We believe in you.

–*Yes, you do. But you can do still more.*

Just what the teacher used to write on our assignments: "Can be improved."

Two days before her death, Françoise asked me if she was going to die. When I said yes, she used an emaciated finger to write in the air, "It's hard." And then she added, "You are strong." "We're talking about your death, Françoise, not mine," I replied. In a certain sense, the death of others is always easier to deal with.

We cried, and then we prayed together, and when it seemed that she was a little more calm, I entrusted two things to her. It was like a cry that came from the depths of my being.

Françoise, I entrust my family to you, and the Community as well (the Community of the Companions, which was already becoming so difficult to manage). Take them with you. I give them to you. Don't forget them.

She nodded yes, twice.

Yes, Lord. I know that you took care of all this, that you answered my prayers, even though I did nothing

to deserve it. One by one, the difficulties we were facing in the Community were smoothed out. The person who wanted to take over the direction of the Community backed off and stopped attacking us. The volunteers and hired staff who joined us to work out their own problems have left. Those who were power hungry, jealous, and spiteful went away on their own. And just as I was on the verge of giving up, having already lost about fifteen pounds, Pierre arrived on the scene. That very day I knew we were saved. I knew it in the very depths of my being when Pierre decided, right after arriving, to keep your real presence here. I was convinced that the most difficult times were behind us. Critical and skeptical friends, whose comments were sometimes very painful, stopped their attacks because we had become "credible" in the eyes of the city. No longer did I have to listen to "Who's looking after the children?" and "Don't forget to take care of yourself," "Don't overdo it," "Don't try to pretend you're one of the poor.". . .

There are still some who don't understand and are waiting for me to start teaching or giving lectures again. It took the presence of the bishop of Chartres and the wife of the governor of the department of Eure-et-Loire at our annual board meeting, along with members of the departmental council from both the right and the left of the political spectrum, to make us (or was it just me?) feel that we had finally arrived. Yes, Lord, this is all true. You were with us. Yes, I do believe.

Today the Lord seems to be asking me, asking us, that this moment not be just a moment, but *that it last.*

October 23

As I walk to the Community we speak to one another.

–Lord, what we are doing for the poor is a mere trifle. What it comes down to at times is little more than a smile or a handshake. That's not very much.

–*You misunderstand.*

–What do you mean?

–*Be intense and light.*

–Intense?

–*Intense in my relationship with you. Live it out intensely. But be light as well, because it is not you who are doing these things; it is I.*

In the evening, at mass in the Hermitage, the Lord comes and takes me in his arms. It's as if I'm wrapped in a thick layer of tenderness. I'm overwhelmed by peace, a sense of presence and pure love.

–Why all this, Lord?

–*So that you may never turn away from me or allow yourself to be turned away.*

Yesterday I drove with a friend to a funeral, and for almost five hours we talked about death and Jesus. He lost his wife two years ago and he's still rebelling against it. I try to tell him about my experience, but it's difficult. His anguish, his honesty, and his rebellion touch me and leave me disabled, a little wounded.

Today it seems that the Lord wants to remind me that it's not up to me to convert people. I'm to stay small, mute at times, but still be present to the suffering of others. If Jesus wants to make the dough rise, he'll do it in his own way.

October 24 (mass at the Companions)

There are several of us. The Lord comes and sits down beside us. His white robe extends to his feet. I'm intrigued by this long, full robe or coat. I tell him so.

–Why are you wearing this?

As so often happens, his reply comes after the Consecration.

–Nicole, do you see how loosely this garment I'm wearing fits me? It's very ample. I'll clothe you with this garment. When you move around, when you walk, you'll feel it on you, brushing against your limbs.

–What do you want to tell us?

–That I move around and that I am alive. You wear me and I am with you.

0

I Am Alive

October 27, 1985 (mass at Batz-sur-mer on the southern coast of Brittany)

Vacation, just me and five kids. The sea is gentle. Our house on the sea is bathed in sunlight. The children are happy and relaxed.

The church where we go for mass is ugly but full. The celebration is lively, and the five children are insufferably cute as they make faces and comment on what is going on. I'm happy to be with them.

Fishnets are suspended from the vaulting of the nave. A large crucifix dominates the church.

I speak to him:

–Lord, why are there so few people who accept you, so few who take advantage of the abundant life that you offer us? All those others. Why don't they come to you?

—I am alive, Nicole. I'm not an abstract idea or a system, but a living person. In order to know me and live with me, you have to choose me, want me.

—Is it a little like choosing a traveling companion?

—Yes. In order to know my light, you have to enter into a relationship with me. It takes two.

October 29 (Batz-sur-mer)

A reading from the Gospel of Saint John 13:17.

As I read these words and live these moments with Jesus, I feel like I'm "one of the family." It's hard to write this lest I turn out to be vain or puffed up with pride. In fact, it's infinitely more simple: I know that I am one of his family, one of his friends. I believe that he had to die in order for me to receive the Holy Spirit so that he could live in me. I understand, not just intellectually but with my whole being, that he had to die. It's absolutely clear to me. Yes, I believe in this man.

I leave the children for a few minutes as they're playing on the rocks and go back to rejoin him in the Batz church. Filled with the memory of the moments I have just relived, I let myself sink into him for a moment.

Then we speak to one another.

—Lord, I know that I'm yours, but I'm still a little afraid.

He knows that I'm afraid, and he knows why. Still I tell him.

—There will be persecutions. You told me so. You told all of us. You also know, Lord, that I need to be "with the world." Ever since I began following you more closely, especially in the company of the Community, you know that there is sometimes a kind of separation

between me "reborn in you" and other people. It scares me a little.

–Don't be afraid. These are nothing but little scratches.

The word *scratches* comes back to me very strongly. I hang on to it even though I don't understand it very well.

As I'm leaving the church Jesus patiently explains it to me.

–When you were little, you took your father's hand, remember? You loved to do it. He reassured you, but still you were a little afraid.

–Yes, I do remember. In fact, I remember something very specific. Once, when we were living in Austria, my father killed a crow – or something that looked like a crow – and he made me pick it up to show me that this ugly beast was harmless. I was afraid to pick it up, so I kept holding on to his hand.

–Your father let go of your hand. That's normal. But now I'm holding your hand, as your father did.

–Lord, you know that I want to show him my notebook. I have wanted to for quite a while. You also know why. May I?

–Yes, you may.

Once again I weep, gently and without sadness.

Friday (mass of the Feast of All Saints, Batz-sur-mer)

In church a lot of people and a lot of singing. Almost too much. It gets in the way. It's hard to encounter him if there isn't any peace and quiet.

His face looms over me. Large, huge. He takes up all the space between the floor and the ceiling of the nave.

–Why are you showing me your face? And why is it so large?

After the Consecration he replies:

–*Because I am alive. I have a face, Nicole, and like all faces, it's animated, expressive; it lives.*

–You mean you smile, you weep, you're sad. . . .

–*Yes. I am alive.*

November 4 (the chapel of the Companions)

Another planet. I'm back at the Community. Everything is whizzing by at a hundred miles an hour. It's not easy to keep up. I'm trying. We have a new director who used to be at an orphanage in Auteuil. The Lord is keeping his promise: I'll make the Community grow. That's what he's doing. I'm happy at heart, even if things are happening so fast here with the Companions that I can't keep up.

At mass I see the image of a man who is standing and loaded down with packages. They're all over the place.

–You see, Lord. It's hard to have to carry so much.

–*Yes. It's hard if you think that you're the only one who's doing the carrying. Believe that I am carrying too, helping you carry. I carry the heaviest things. I help you.*

November 5 (mass at the chapel)

There are a lot of us. Some Companions are in front of me. They sit there, stooped over, their hands all muddy, and not exactly smelling of Chanel No. 5. Those assigned to read the lessons stumble through them. My heart is touched at the sight of such poverty, and yet I can't keep myself from asking him:

–Are these really the people you prefer? Why is that?

–They haven't built up any fortresses, any barricades, around themselves. They haven't used their intelligence to construct a system against me.

As I walk toward the Community, I reflect on some phrases from the Gospel:

–Lord, it's strange that you should say this to us. I believe that everything – friendship, love – is based on mutuality. I'm not talking about giving for the sake of getting something back, but still, you can't just give or just receive.

–You're right, Nicole. When you give to a poor person who is unable to repay you, I'll repay you, because it's to me that you gave.

November 7 (mass at the Community)

There are quite a few of us. Companions and some friends. The Lord comes to tell us:

–Don't be afraid. In your shortsightedness, you let yourselves be weighed down by all you have to do, by your cares and problems, by tomorrow and yesterday. Don't be afraid. You have to go beyond all that. I can see farther than you. I know.

From the beginning of mass, Jesus, who is seated alongside me, has held me to his heart. I felt good leaning against him, but sad at the same time since I felt myself weighed down by all my responsibilities at home and elsewhere and by the fact that Pierre is going to be leaving soon to preach a retreat. Without him around it's hard to manage, but I'm happy that he's going to do what he's made for, namely, to speak about his relationship with the Jesus he follows.

–And that's why you're holding me so close to you, Lord. You know all this.

–Yes, I do. Don't be afraid. I am alive. I want you to sense it, and that is why I'm holding you so close to me.

November 10 (the chapel)

Jesus kneels and holds my face in his hands.

–Why are you doing this, Lord?

–I want you to sense that I am alive. Give me the gift of believing that I am alive, that I protect you and go before you.

Tomorrow Pierre is going away and leaving me at the helm of this double community, the Hermitage and the center here in town. I already know that it's not going to be easy.

November 12 (the Community)

As I expected, Pierre is hardly gone and he has left a storm behind him and a great void.

The storm erupts over the rivalry between two staff members. All hell breaks loose. The three of us get together and put our cards on the table. I listen. One is angry, the other hurt. I'm calm inside. I intervene very little, but I do so firmly. I remind them that we are here to work together. The storm abates. One of them asks the other for pardon. My heart leaps for joy. A few minutes later we take Communion together with some Companions. I can't get over the sense of peace! It was a true gift. The hands holding my face were truly his.

November 13 (in town)

It's Wednesday today, and that means my little family gets to monopolize its mother. Nothing unusual about that. A short visit from the friend of a friend who be-

longs to an Orthodox Church. Her intelligence and, above all, her spirituality bring a warm glow to the house and to some guests of ours. And then I have to run off to the Companions. When I arrive I'm a little out of breath. One of the Companions is there.

–We were waiting for you. Are you going to say the mass?

–No, Jean-Pierre.

I explain that what we had yesterday was a Communion service, and that today and hereafter, while Pierre is away, we will have a half-hour period of adoration.

–No problem, he says. It's all the same to me.

And so all four of us remained there, three Companions and I, before the Lord in silence. The silence was real. Such a gift. I thank the Lord.

–*I will make you a queen,* he replies.

And then a few moments later:

–*Take me into yourself. Let me fill all the space within you.*

His hands touch my face. Of course I say yes. How could I refuse?

–I don't deserve any of this, Lord. I feel completely satisfied and still surprised. What do you want to do in me?

–*I want to expand in you.*

–And I? What am I to do?

–*Enter into yourself to ask me what you should do. Question me within yourself. Don't act, don't reflect from the outside. Enter into yourself to question me.*

The Lord is unbelievable!

This evening I asked him to send workers into the harvest, to enlarge our Community and establish it in the city.

–There is too much misery in the streets. Please do something, Lord.

November 14 (the chapel, adoration)

–*I am here. Let me work through you.*

–What do you mean?

–*Within this Community and for this Community, act and live as if you were expecting everything from me. Don't plan anything, except what depends on you.*

–But, Lord, we have some situations here that are not very easy to deal with. You know that better than I.

–*I'll answer you, I'll tell you what you should say at the time you need it. Don't worry about anything.*

November 15 (the chapel)

A full day, but a peaceful one. At the Hermitage the entire team is working. Florent, the new associate director, and I are given a warm welcome. The work is going ahead very well. I thank the Lord for all these smiling faces and for the proposals we have talked about.

Pierre isn't here this evening. Every Friday he speaks to them about this man "Jesus." I'll have to take his place. On my knees in the chapel I tell the Lord about my fear.

–I'm too intellectual for them, Lord. Help me to "speak" you.

I open the Bible and the passage given me is the one about Mary Magdalene with the gardener in front of the stone that has been rolled away. I spoke. It was relatively easy. I feel like Mary Magdalene, amazed at such love, such sensitivity and tenderness.

A few minutes later, I'm in the chapel for a period of adoration.

—*I will make this Community grow. Don't ask me where, when, or how. I'll do it.*

—What about me, Lord? What am I to do?

—*You are to let me work through you. And I will.*

Sunday, November 17 (mass at the Carmel)

I speak to him before going to mass and at the beginning of the mass.

—Lord, one of my relatives is mean and belligerent. She's having a hard time, Lord. And the twenty-two thousand who were killed when that volcano erupted in Colombia. It's just dreadful, Lord.

—*Yes, I know.*

—Say something. Speak to me.

—*If your relative is feeling depressed or a catastrophe happens at the other end of the world, there is really nothing you can do. It's beyond you. You're not able to do anything about it. So let it go.*

—But if I let it go, that means I'm running away from it. It's like saying, since it's not my fault, I can forget about it.

—*No, you're not running away. You're being like me. You're sharing the suffering, and you're praying.*

—I'm sorry, but to me that sounds like running away.

—*No. Do what depends on you.*

—What is that?

—*Pray and give me shelter.*

—You want to take shelter in me?

—*Yes, I want to stay with you, live in you.*

—Why?

—*To do what you can't do by yourself. I'll do it. I'm the only one who can do it.*

Yes, I do understand what the Lord wants to tell me. He will do what I can't do, provided I give him space.

—I think I understand what you want to tell me. But why do you want to come and stay with me? It's not always very nice in here. I'm really amazed that you'd choose me as a place to do the work of building your kingdom.

—*But why not, Nicole? After all, I was born in a barn.*

Amen, Lord. And even though I'm usually so sensitive, I'm not at all miffed to learn that I'm not a five-star hotel! Move in. I will proclaim your marvels.

Monday, November 18 *(adoration in the chapel)*

There are five of us: Florent, our new associate director, and three Companions. Jesus is here.

—Thank you, Lord, for everything you're giving this Community. I marvel a bit that Florent and the Companions are here.

—*Didn't I tell you? Didn't I promise you? I'll do even more. Let me walk ahead of you. Don't be afraid. I'm going to give you more.*

—Thank you, Lord. It's true that I'm now putting you on right side out. Am I wearing you correctly now?

—*Yes.*

—And you want this clothing to keep me warm so that I really feel you?

—*Yes.*

—And that's why you're spoiling me so much?

—*Yes.*

Tuesday, November 19

A busy day at home and a lot of activity at the Community. Two contentious hoodlums show up, and it's hard for me to stay calm. A eucharistic service this evening in the chapel. We had been using a construction hut for a chapel, but now we need it to house two men. Delicately we move the Blessed Sacrament (the Lord) to a smaller hut. Only half of the hut has been cleaned. We follow him and place him in the clean part. Our sharing is impressive. One of the Companions tells us about his suffering. It's very moving. The Lord speaks to us.

–*Be really united among yourselves. I am the bond between you. Brothers and sisters. Don't be afraid.*

This evening, prayer with the Bon Secours sisters. There are ten of us, including a priest. The Lord speaks a lot and uses me a lot as well. I used to be afraid to lead prayer in the presence of all these "professionals," but now I feel not only confident but peaceful.

November 20 (in the somewhat cramped chapel of the Companions)

There are five of us.

–*I will increase this Community. I will continue to act. Don't be afraid.*

–I believe you, Lord, and I'm not even concerned to know where, when, and with whom. I just believe you'll do it. I'm going to try to leave you the biggest place.

–*Yes. Do your work well. Don't worry. I'll do it with you.*

–Greater things than I could do alone? Is that sort of it?

—*Yes.*

—I know why, Lord. Because I'm two. There are two of us working for your kingdom. You have passed through death, Lord, so that everyone who believes in you may be two.

—*Yes.*

November 21 (the chapel)

I look at his face. It's the same face as on the Holy Shroud.

—Your death must have been dreadful, Lord: such affliction, such anguish.

—*Yes.*

—Even with your Father who loved you and whom you loved, it was dreadful.

—*Yes, but it had to be. And now you also know that you have to pass through death in order to find hope. I had to give you that hope.*

—Yes, Jesus. It's truly a cross. But now you can act in us and with us because you have been victorious once and for all.

—*Yes.*

—But how they have disfigured your cross and your message, Lord.

—*Yes.*

November 22 (adoration)

—*Don't be afraid. I'll do it for you, for all of you, for this Community.*

I'm reassured as he touches my face with his hands.

November 23 (*adoration*)

It was a difficult day. One of the Companions who used to pray with us regularly started drinking again and has become miserable and aggressive.

It's tough. His anguish is more painful to me than his hostility. Our future associate director is present, close by. He lets himself be struck and says nothing. The Companion leaves. I cry.

–He's so miserable, Lord.

–*Yes, I know.*

–Talk to me.

–*You know how I feel every time you turn your backs on me and refuse me. You know. His anguish is the same as mine. I'm part of it, Nicole.*

–Lord, you force me to look at myself, my own failings, my own turning away, and yet you tell me that you're ready to take me back in your arms again. Is that right?

–*Yes.*

November 24 (*a sharing at the Hermitage*)

Two staff, four Companions. I divide the host. Jesus is here, minuscule but living.

–Tell me, Lord, what is the link between human distress and your own love? How far apart are they?

–*I'll take you from floor to floor. Don't stay on the ground floor. Don't be content with a shortsighted view. The house that I'm giving you to live in has several stories. Don't be satisfied with the basement.*

–Will you show me the other levels?

–*Yes.*

November 28 (mass at the chapel)

Pierre is back. With him present, I can handle anything with the Companions. The burden is infinitely lighter. There is a song in my heart, and the sadness of the past three days gives way to happiness.

–I'm happy, Jesus.

–*Yes, I know. I'm sharing it.*

–You really are alive.

–*Yes. Yesterday you and I shared your sorrow. Today I'm rejoicing with you.*

And then, after praying in tongues:

–*Don't press me. I'll take care of it. I'll enlarge the Community. Don't be afraid.*

The Hermitage (the chapel)

After the Consecration:

–Where do I live in this house you have spoken about, Lord?

–*You live on the first floor. But really live in it. You have things to do. Do them well.*

–You mean my daily tasks, the nuisances, decisions, telephone calls, projects?

–*Yes. Do them well.*

–Who lives on the second floor?

–*Those you hear walking overhead, over your heart sometimes. Those who press you, get in your way every now and then.*

–What should I do about them?

–*Listen to them, Nicole. Listen to the sounds they make. Don't seal yourself off from them.*

–What do you mean by that?

—You don't have to move in with them or live with them. Live on your own floor, but listen to the sounds they make. Don't forget them.

Mass with my family, Saint Aignan

—Lord, I have to love and help those who live above me. Both of us have to listen to them.

—Yes.

—But without wanting to do everything for them or live with them, right?

—Yes.

—And above them, Jesus? Who lives above them?

—Those whom I have in reserve to help you, love you, guide you.

—Do I know them?

—No, not all of them. But I know them and I'm preparing them for you, for the others, and for the Community.

In fact, the Lord has always provided me with hands and hearts when things became too difficult, when I had to undertake a new venture or overcome difficulties. Thank you.

Mass at the regional reunion of graduates of the Saint Cyr Military Academy

There are about twenty of us. We pray for those who have died and in whose memory we have come together today.

After the Consecration:

—Who lives on the top floor?

—The multitude of those who are already with me and who are ready to help you.

Philippe's parents, Françoise, Jean-Luc, and so many others. I call on them.

–*They are not that far away. They are among the living, Nicole. You have to believe that.*

A little later:

–We don't go to you all by ourselves, Lord. We have to go to you with the whole house, with all the floors of it.

–*Yes.*

December 3 (mass at the chapel)

A marvelous respite with the Lord after a pretty exhausting day. Shopping and housecleaning in the morning, lunch with a friend who is suffering from depression, monthly conferences with each of the Companions.

I'm heartened by this peace that draws me into the Lord.

–Thank you, Lord. I'm always surprised and amazed that you choose to come and live in me.

–*Do a good job of getting the straw ready for me. That's all I need. Something simple. Don't welcome me with too many decorations and trimmings. Just your heart.*

7

0

Don't Be
Afraid

December 6, 1985 (Cathedral of Saint John, Lyons)

The cathedral is full of children and Marist priests who
have come together for a traditional Marian celebration.
I feel a little out of place in this community. A simple
and prayerful tone is set right at the beginning of the
celebration. The Gospel of the angel telling Mary that
she will be a mother makes my heart leap. Almost every
word affects me as if I were Mary and as if the angel
were speaking to me. I try to pull myself together but
don't succeed. I feel as if I'm sinking, drowning. I'm not
going to pretend that I'm the Virgin Mary. Am I going
crazy? The experience is so strong that I'm not able to
hold back my tears.

And then Mary comes toward me. She's dressed in
blue, accompanied by her Son. She points to him and
humbly tells me:

–He needs you. My Son needs you.

This is way too much for me. I feel that I'm founder-
ing, and in a panic I ask Jesus:

–Speak to me. Give me a sign. Show me that I'm not
dreaming, that I'm not going crazy.

The priest gets up to give the sermon. He's a simple
man, and everyone appears to love him, especially the
children.

–At this moment, the Lord is speaking to your
hearts. He's asking you to follow him. Listen to him.

His sermon is a love poem, a love poem winging up
to God.

I'm not crazy. Jesus wants me to be his servant. He
wants Mary's yes. He wants me to be like Mary.

–Lord, look at me. Look at my limitations, look at
what you're asking of me. You want us to expand the
Community, but there are so few of us. It's a heavy load
for Pierre and me. And yet you want us to expand?

–*Yes.*

A little later I said yes. It was the humble yes of a
servant. All I'm sure of is my goodwill.

Fiat – so be it.

December 10 (the chapel)

Communion service. There are ten of us in our little
chapel. The room is filled with our songs and prayers.
Jesus is there, happy to see us together.

December 11 (the chapel)

Adoration. The Companions and I in our corner. The
tenderness of Jesus surrounds us.

December 12, 13, 14, 15

Things are happening fast. At home. With the Companions. The two planets on which I live are hard to handle. Philippe has been exhausted for the past two weeks; the kids are on edge with the approach of Christmas; a friend criticizes me harshly for being too liberal; I have to take charge of the annual board meeting. . . . It's way too much. I'm doing my best to live in the present moment. But it's very difficult for me "truly" to be present on these two planets that are so different from each other. A mini-tempest hits, in me first, and then with a friend. Everything seems to be intent on upsetting my equilibrium.

Mass at the chapel: a moment of peace.

–*The sea is rough, Nicole. I am here.*

–Where, Lord?

–*Look at me. I am the rope that you see. Be the buoy in the sea.*

The image is that of a storm-tossed sea with a buoy bobbing to and fro. The buoy is me.

–Why, Lord?

–*That's how I want you. I want others to see you.*

–And what's to become of me?

–*You'll hold on to me.*

–Where are you?

–*The rope that comes down from the sky and secures the buoy. Hold on to me.*

The storm didn't let up. It lasted through a whole sleepless night of intense struggle.

Calm was finally restored the next evening. I have the impression that evil forces were making sport of me and using me as a plaything.

–Why, Lord? You know how hard I fought. Why?

–*You were not holding onto the rope – to me – tight enough. You knew it was there, but you really didn't come and hold on to it.*

I think about it, and he's right.

–Next time I'll try, Lord. I promise you. I'll try harder.

He smiles.

I'm completely beat. I'll sleep soundly tonight.

December 16 and following . . .

Full days. Pierre is worn out. Another bout of multiple sclerosis. He hears in only one ear. He still has a smile and a kind word for everyone, but I feel sorry for him. Philippe is also beat. He's had a battery of tests. Nothing serious, but every now and then he gets run-down. Laurette is sick, and though it's not serious, she has to spend two days in bed. In the middle of all this I keep on going, happy to get gifts ready for the family and all the Companions. Taking care of a thousand and one details and being on hand for everybody leaves me completely exhausted when evening rolls around. And yet the Lord wants us to expand!

–You know all this, Lord. Are you sure about what you're telling us?

–*Yes.*

–Look at my limitations. Look at what you're asking of me.

–*Nicole, I'll carry you. I'll carry you like a babe in my arms. Let go.*

–What about Pierre?

–*I'm holding him to my heart. Don't be afraid. I have him tightly in my arms.*

The next day at the chapel, mass

–Have faith. All of you, have faith. Be like me.

–It's hard.

–Nicole, I was born in a stable and died on a cross. What more do you want? What greater proof of my love do you need? Nicole, I need your trust. I need you to be like a little servant. I'll make you a queen, Nicole. I'm already doing it.

–You're right, Lord. I can tell. But are you really asking me to do nothing? Do you simply want us to let ourselves be carried by you?

–Yes.

–What about all the others?

–They'll look at you and all the rest, and they'll follow us. When they see us – Pierre and me, you and me, the Community and me – they'll come to me.

December 24

All sorts of last-minute shopping to take care of with Laurette sick in bed. This evening we are going to join my family in Rambouillet. Before leaving, I drop in at the hall where the Secours Catholique is hosting a meal for more than three hundred people. The poor are there. We say hello. We know one another. As I'm leaving I see someone silhouetted in the dark coming toward the door. I feel uneasy. At the last minute I recognize Jean-Yves. He's drunk and there's hatred in his eyes. I leave; the family is waiting for me. Later on I found out that he got into a fight with the director of the Secours Catholique and that the demonic force in him was so strong it took four people to subdue him. Pierre came and prayed, and Jean-Yves immediately

calmed down and began to cry. The demons left him, for the time being at least.

Christmas with my family was calm and peaceful. At the Companions there were eighteen for mass, and when we gave presents the next day, there was a look of tenderness in the eyes of those broken men.

End of December, beginning of January 1986

There's so much to do. In the evening I'm too tired to write. I need peace and quiet to write down what he tells us.

It's heavy going right now. The tribe is tired, on edge. The little patience I have gets used up quickly by the care I have to take not to step on anyone's toes. I'm afraid that I'm not keeping my priorities in order. I'm worried about the future of the Community, and I tell him so.

–*Don't be afraid. The preparations for your party have already been taken care of. I have already set the table.*

I see an immense white tablecloth.

–Why this image, Lord?

. –*So that you may sense deep inside that I'm already waiting for you. Don't be afraid.*

The next day the image is sharper. My table is set and I feel deep down that Jesus wants to tell me that his kingdom has already begun here below. That I don't have anything to fear.

The next day he receives me with wide-open arms. A light so strong it's almost blinding seems to radiate from them. I draw near, but the light is so intense that I can't enter into it completely.

–*It's too soon. It's too strong for you. Wait. You'll see.*

Something incredible happens the next day. After the Consecration a light settles on my face. It seems as if I'm illuminated, bathed in immense softness. And I hear these unbelievable words:

–*You're beautiful. I love you like this.*

I have to say it again: it's unbelievable.

(By the way, I forgot to say that one of the Companions, whom I trusted, has taken off with my car, my papers, etc. I keep my calm. This isn't the first time one of them has betrayed our confidence, nor will it be the last. I find this theft infinitely easier to take than the insults or the hatred of some of the others.)

And then, on Sunday, water damage in the house. The library got it. My favorite room. The ceiling has to be repaired, books are ruined. . . . I have a good cry. I guess I'm not as "unattached" as I thought!

January 9 (mass at the Companions)

We pray for those who are absent, for my thief, for those who have left us. We are at peace.

After the Consecration, the Lord says to us:

–*Don't be upset. Let me get into your boat. I'll guide it. Let me get in and you'll not be afraid of anything.*

–The sea is always rough, Lord.

–*Yes, but with me in your boat, you don't have to be afraid of anything. I'll be here with you in the storm. I'll protect you.*

January 10

–*Make the most of the moment I give you. Don't sell the present short. Live fully in the here and now; I'll take care of*

tomorrow. Don't let yourself be weighed down by worrying about the future. I'll act.

All these days in January have been difficult, so harried that I haven't even been able to write every evening. First of all, there's Philippe, who is worn out and ill. It's been dragging on for a month. Ever since the beginning of January I feel I've been pulled in all directions for the sake of the Community. I feel that I'm being used for everything and for nothing. It's difficult and I'm tired.

This evening my heart is in turmoil. Philippe is completely spent. I'm anxious about his sunken appearance. I'm not going to Algeria to hike on the Ahaggar plateau, even though it's a respite that I was so looking forward to. Benoît is a full-fledged teenager and rejects his mother: nothing unusual about that, but still difficult for me to accept.

Mass at the Hermitage. I try not to cry, but I can't take it anymore.

–Lord, I'm on my knees. I've had it. Surely you see how heavy my burden is.

–Yes, I know.

And then, without speaking, he comes toward me and stretches out his arms to me.

–Don't be upset. I know. I'm going to help you.

The next day, I feel a little better, but I still have a hard time making any headway.

–I'm helping you walk. I'm beside you.

The evening is pure anguish. Philippe got inconclusive results on his blood test, and now I wait for two hours for the doctor's verdict. All I can do is wait. Minute by minute, I get on with what I have to do. The children, the soup, the telephone. . . . The doctor says

there is nothing to worry about, and Laurette is surprised at how calm I was. My heart beat wildly, but I was being helped.

January 19 (mass with the Companions)

—*I grasp you by the shoulders. I am your companion. I am really here.*

—Why is that, Lord?

—*You need it. You need to feel my tenderness and my love for you.*

This evening at mass his presence was so overpowering that I almost collapsed.

January 20

—*Rejoice to have me for your shepherd. Be happy.*

January 21

—*Say yes to me. Not "yes but," but "YES." A real yes.*

January 21

Mass: David and Goliath.

—*Be like David. Fight with the arms that I give you, with what you are. Don't look for any other protection but me. I'll help you.*

January 23 and following . . .

The sea is storm-tossed. Philippe needs to be hospitalized for a week. We have to find a place in Paris. I feel

bad for him, and of course I'm worried, but I'm not distraught. I'm determined to live in the present, and I'm managing to do that because I really feel that I'm being helped. I'm sleeping normally and trying to do well what needs to be done. Jesus accompanies me, attentive and kind. I sense him at the Eucharist, of course, but also in the calm I feel in spite of myself. He knows what he's doing. And so I hold his hand firmly.

On the twenty-fifth of January, after the Eucharist, his face is next to mine. I'm infused with an ineffable sweetness and tenderness. His face is like a beam of light that goes through every part of me, leaving me in great peace.

–Do you have something to tell me?

–*I'm here. I want you to feel me. I'm living in you, around you, through you.*

–Thank you.

January 26

I feel so relaxed after Communion that I almost drop off to sleep. I have to struggle to stay awake.

January 27

The Lord asks us to bring him our gifts, as the three kings did.

–What gifts are you talking about, Jesus? I'm not rich, nor is the Community.

–*Bring me what you are.*

I give him these difficult days, these comings and goings between the Community, home, the drugstore, the lab . . . to say nothing of the sempiternal shopping

trips to make sure that the family has food on the table twice a day.

He accepts it all. I'm sure of it.

January 28

—Stretch yourself out on my tenderness, on my love. I love you. That's understood.

January 30

—I am a companion. I walk ahead of you, but I go slow in order to walk with you. Follow me. I am the road.

February 2

After the Consecration, the Lord seems to lift up both my hands in order to draw me to himself. My face is bathed in light and power.

—I want you to feel my presence.

February 3

The Lord asks us to welcome all people and everything that happens.

—Continue to welcome.

February 4

—Look at me. Look at my face. I know that the road is rocky. Don't look down at your feet.

8

No "Yes, But"

February 5, 1986

The first burial. At the hospital. It's poor and barren: not even a flower. We are burying the brother of one of the Companions. The poor and the homeless are there, about fifteen of them. Secours Catholique is present too. Pierre, the Companions.

The Lord enters the church and seems to take us all in his arms.

—Be joyful. You are rich in me.

Later on there is the funeral, without mass, of a month-old baby. The mother is in anguish. The pain that the others are suffering affects me deeply. But the baby is among the living.

At the Hermitage

—Don't put your trust in yourselves. Put it in me. You have me inside you like a buried treasure. Entrust yourselves to me. Do what you have to do, but lean on me.

At the Community, Eucharist

Beams of light seem to shine forth from his open hands.

—I pour out my tenderness on you. Let it wash over you.

It's like a great light, a sweetness that floods us.

—This light isn't going to melt away your difficulties. It will not make the cross you're carrying disappear. It envelops everything. Believe in my tenderness.

—I do believe in it, Jesus.

February 19

—Where are you, Lord?

No answer.

A few minutes later the back of my neck begins to feel warm. It's like a bright point centered on a spot on my neck. I'm suspicious at first. I rub my hand over the spot. There's nothing there, and yet I feel this warmth until the end of mass.

—What's this all about?

—I want you to feel me.

February vacation

There are twelve of us in the group. On the very first day I break my wrist.

—I think I'm going to have a lot of time to spend with you, Jesus.

He smiles.

February 22

I come and kneel before him, with him, in a little chapel in Abriès while the rest of the group goes skiing in the Alps.

    —Continue to be my little servant. Let me work through you.

February 23

The little chapel is closed. I walk along a snow-covered path. We speak to each other.

    —Why are you always calling me "little servant"?

    —I want you to take care of the others.

    —Are you the one who will do that in me?

    —Yes. Let it happen.

February 24

On a snow-covered road made brilliant by the sun.

    —"Little servant"? Explain that some more.

    —Like Mary. Be like her.

Is that all! The Lord has pretty high hopes!

    —"Little." The word sounds positive. Tell me more.

    —Little servant and queen of my heart.

What a way of life! The words shock me. Tears spring to my eyes. Tomorrow he will explain it to me more fully.

February 25

I have been walking in the snow for an hour all by myself in silence. He tells me what he means by "queen of my heart."

    —"Little" and "queen of my heart"?

—That means that you will touch my heart. I will be touched *by the things you will say to me.*

—!!! I'll be able to ask you for absolutely anything?

—No, Nicole. Little. You will be like a belt that transmits power from one pulley to another. It will not be you who does the asking, but the others through you.

February 26 (once again on the road)

I look at a rushing torrent. Here and there it's blocked by piles of snow.

—Little. That's what you're seeing, Nicole.

—The flowing water is clear and strong.

—Yes. Take a good look at it.

The snow on the two banks keeps the water from spreading out over the whole riverbed.

—Do you see, Nicole? Being little means allowing your- self to be channeled by me. Don't spread yourself out. Let yourself be channeled, and like the torrent you will be much more powerful.

It seems that the Lord wants me to keep the water clear. He will see to it that it runs swiftly.

—You want people to see both the clarity and the power of the torrent. You want me to be like this moun- tain stream?

—Yes.

—That's what I want, too, but I'm not worthy.

—Just wait. You'll see.

February 27

I'm still taking walks in these mountains that are almost too white. Suddenly I realize that I don't hear the tor- rent any more.

—*Bury yourself as it did. Bury yourself in me.*

—What you want me to do, Jesus, is draw my strength from you, with you?

—*Yes.*

Friday

The Way of the Cross in a little chapel along with four old women from the area. After each station they race through their Our Father's and Hail Mary's. It makes me dizzy, and the speed, which is almost offensive, gets on my nerves.

—They're not speaking to you, Lord. They're just turning out prayers.

He smiles and says nothing.

—And all this gloom, Lord. It's really depressing.

Still no reply. And then I realize that I'm very spoiled because I spend my life with someone who is truly alive. The way of the cross is *behind,* not ahead. I'm definitely very spoiled. I feel like a little child with an enormous Christmas present in her arms. The present is so big that I can hardly handle it. I really do have to let go.

March (back to the Companions, at the chapel)

The Lord asks me to be joyful. A little earlier, during a funeral mass for the mother of a friend of our children, the Lord had already asked me to be joyful. She died after an eleven-year struggle against cancer and left a fifteen-year-old son. To all appearances it's absurd.

—I feel so awful for this child, and you ask me to be joyful.

–Yes. In my loving gaze, in my gaze that sees you as you are, that creates and shapes you each day, be joyful.

March 4

He tells me once again to be joyful. To be happy to live with him and by him.

–Be transparent, too.

This is a living bond that he offers me. There's nothing platonic about it.

March 6 and 7

I'm reading *Prison to Praise* by Merlin R. Carothers. It's very American, a little simplistic. Saying thank you in any and all circumstances rubs me the wrong way, and yet I talk to the Lord about it.

–To me, each and every thank you is unique.

–Lord, I simply cannot say thank you for the nails they drove into your hands. It's not possible.

He smiles.

–Could you explain it to me, Lord?

–I'll teach you another way.

–Start right now.

–Through it all, Nicole. I am "with you through it all." Giles in the hospital with cancer, Lucette and her child who is undergoing psychiatric therapy, Martine and her husband who is withdrawing more and more. I know all that. Weep with them. Yes. Suffer with them, Nicole, but through it all tell them that I am present, that I am there through it all.

–I don't see anything. I'll have to make this act of faith in total darkness.

–Don't allow yourself to be completely swallowed up by

*your compassion. Save a place for me. Let me suffer with
you. I am there, too.*

March 13 (Eucharist at the chapel)

The back of my neck feels heavy, as if someone were
pressing on it from above. The pressure is strong, but it
doesn't hurt. Once again, I have the impression that I'm
sinking.

—What are you trying to tell me, Jesus?

—*Be little, obedient.*

—When I'm relaxed like this, I feel fine. Like this,
things seem easy.

—*Let go, let me do it. I want you to sense that obedience
will make you happy and at ease.*

March 16 (Sunday mass at Saint Aignan)

I see the face of the Lord, immense and smiling.

—*I have taken everything unto myself, have absorbed
everything. Don't be afraid. I'm here.*

March 18 (chapel of the Companions)

This morning, while shopping, I see two Companions
at a sidewalk café. They should have been back two
days ago.

—Lord, what we're doing is so trifling. We're not able
to hold on to them. Sooner or later they all go back to
drink. It hurts.

—*It's not your Community, Nicole. It's mine.*

At that very moment, I let go of everything. I
handed it all over to him. He knows better than I.

That evening at chapel:

–*I'll place my love in your heart. I'll come and love in you. Don't be afraid.*

–What about me? I'm not to do anything? Just be passive? That's pretty negative, Lord.

–*No, you're to stay little and obedient. Take people and things as I give them to you and then . . . let me handle it.*

Saint-Benoît-sur-Loire

A mini-retreat of not quite two full days. Concelebrated mass in the basilica. The Gospel: Mary pours precious perfume on the feet of Jesus.

–*Do what she did.*

–You want me to sit at your feet, to take time for you?

–*Yes. And more than that. I want you to spoil me.*

–You certainly do spoil me, Lord. And I'd like to try to spoil you. But I don't have anything precious to offer you.

–*I need you to spoil me.*

–What do I have that's precious and that I can pour out on you?

–*Your trust, your childlike trust. Make that your gift to me.*

I see, or rather I sense what he means. He doesn't want a few isolated acts of confidence, but wants my faith in him to be poured out freely and continuously.

Later, as I'm alone with him in the oratory, feeling warm and comfortable, I entrust to him the sufferings of those who are in my care, the Community of the Companions, the difficult ones. I'm at his feet. Both of us are happy.

The oratory, Saint-Benoît-sur-Loire

I'm seated at his feet.

—Lord, I give you my trust. But, you know, it's easy today; tomorrow will be more difficult. It's not clear how one can be caught up in the messiness of everyday life and still remain faithful to you.

—*No "yes, but." Give me this trust without any holding back.*

—It's yours.

An instant of communion. He raises his face to me and surrounds me with his light like a lover.

—Do you want us to be two and one at the same time?

—*Yes. I want to become your breathing. We will breathe together.*

Oh la la! I wonder if the Lord isn't going a little too far.

—Do you really want to live in me?

—*Yes.*

—What is it you love in me?

—*You're fresh and calm.*

—Not always, Lord. Far from it. You know how unbearable and headstrong I can be.

—*Yes, I know.*

And he smiles.

Such love, such love for the little wisp of a woman that I am, is completely beyond my understanding.

—Do you really need me?

—*Yes.*

I still feel like arguing, and so I do. I tell him again that I need Philippe, Pierre, Bernard . . . that I need human hands and human love if I'm to keep going.

He's a little pained as he answers me:

–*I have always spoiled you. I have always given you those hands. What makes you think I'm going to stop now?*

I sense, sense deeply, that if I succeed in living and breathing with him, only the present moment will count. Fears, suffering, worry will no longer amount to anything.

–Help me, Jesus. I want the promise I make to you today to be more than just a flash in the pan. See to it that when difficulty comes my way I don't try to go it alone and leave you off to the side. If I go on my way without you, catch me quickly. I know that it's only in this way that your kingdom will advance. Yes, Lord, we will breathe together. That's what I want.

The beginning of April

These past days have been somewhat hard. Having my arm in a cast bothers me, but it's too painful to go without the cast. On top of that I've had an abscess and a tooth extracted. The sky is as gray as the month of November, and the wind is so cold that you need your winter coat and boots. I feel heavy, shriveled up.

Pierre is away, but the Community is getting along pretty well.

Sunday (mass at Saint Aignan)

–I'm here to see you, Lord. I haven't been very attentive to you.

–*I was waiting for you.*

Just the hint of a reprimand.

April 7 (at the chapel of the Companions)

I take time to spend a half hour with him by myself. The chapel is cold and deserted in Pierre's absence.

–It's good to be with you, Lord.

And it's true. He warms my heart. I hear the Companions calling to one another, the door banging. I hear the sounds of life outside, but at the same time I sense another life within me.

–Why am I ignoring you a little right now, Lord, even though I know you are the true life? I don't just know it, I savor it.

–*I am life to the full. The road I offer you is full of light. You will walk in pools of light.*

–Then why am I holding back a little? Tell me.

–*Because you want to know things ahead of time.*

–What things?

–*The gifts that I'm giving you: my peace, my joy, my liberty.*

–And what's wrong with that?

–*You can't. You imagine these gifts in relation to your own experience, according to what you know about peace and joy and light. But my peace, the peace that I am giving you, comes from me. You can't know it, because it's other.*

–I imagine it to be immense and profound.

–*It is life to the full. You can only come to know it by letting go.*

April 8 (in the chapel)

A quiet day, on the whole. I take some time to rest with the Lord.

–This chapel is cold, Lord, and those Companions who used to be with us for the Eucharist have started drinking again. That hurts.

–*The point is not their fidelity, but* yours.

–How can you say that, Lord? We were in this to-gether. You want us to be your witnesses, don't you?

–*A witness, yes. I want you to be a little servant and a witness to the light.*

April 9 (chapel of the Hermitage)

Alone in his presence in this cold chapel, I try to forget about the day, about the suicidal Companion that I have just been listening to, in order to enter into communion with him.

–Today's been tough.

–*Be sure of me.*

–What do you mean?

He repeats:

–*Be sure of me, unconditionally sure of me.*

–Tell me what you mean.

–*Be sure of me independently of the circumstances I give you to live through, the people you meet, the pleasant or difficult situations in which you find yourself. Be sure of me, enriched by me, regardless of what may come.*

April 12 (mass at the chapel of the Companions)

The Gospel of a couple of loaves of bread and some fish that fed a whole crowd. This Gospel is meant for us today.

–These few loaves of bread are so trifling, Lord. And I have the impression that what we're doing here for the Companions is trifling, too.

There are only three of us at the Eucharist. Yesterday we were two. The Companions who used to take part in

this meal have left and have returned to drink, to the street, to misery.

   –*Believe in the trifling. I give the increase. I do the multiplying.*

April 14 (Le Queyras)

A few days of vacation, just Philippe and me. At last! I find the torrent from last February again, but this time the snow is gone and the stream is wide and shallow.

   –There's a season for everything, isn't there, Lord? Now it's spring. It's the same torrent, but how different it is from last winter.

   –*Don't be in a hurry. Be like the water of this stream. Give yourself over to me.*

   –In other words?

   –*Let yourself be channeled, guided by me. Be like the stream; don't go too fast. Accept these days when it seems that nothing or very little is happening in the Community. I'm preparing you, getting you ready for tomorrow. You don't see much. The stream is under the snow. But I'm on the job, busy at work.*

   –It's true. You're helping me, helping us, to mature.

   –*Yes. Allow me to work through you.*

April 15 (Le Queyras)

The snow, the silence, and the repose are like a cocoon for me. I thank Jesus for this peaceful time with Philippe. It's such a gift.

   –*Keep on letting go.*

The image of water and a torrent returns.

—Don't confuse "letting go" with passivity. Be joyful and clear like this water, without worrying about where I'm taking you. Don't be impatient. I know where I'm leading you.

—I want to ask you where.

—Why do you want to know? Are you afraid? Don't you trust me?

April 16

Philippe has left for the mountains, and I come to spend a few moments with Jesus. As a way of placing myself in his presence, I often begin by saying "thank you" (thank you for Philippe, the children, this place, etc.), and then I slowly recite the words of the Our Father and the Hail Mary. Both Jesus and Mary are present and they're happy to see me like this. All is well.

—Talk to me, Jesus. I'm sure you have something to say to me again today.

—Yes. Do you remember when I mentioned the second breath?

—Yes.

—It's easier than you think. Let go. Not just of a part of yourself, but of your whole self.

—Tell me what you mean.

—It's like when you swim. Your whole body goes forward in the water. Let yourself be completely carried by the current. Don't cling to the shore, don't go against the current.

—So what you're proposing isn't some kind of passivity.

—No, not at all. I'm talking about obedience. You follow the current without knowing where it will lead you, because you know how good it feels to let yourself be carried by the water. Just to swim.

–Why, Jesus?
–*So that the world will see me.*

April 17

Today the message is very simple. The image is still that of the torrent.

–*Don't be afraid. The water carries you. I carry you.*

April 18 (on my knees)

–I am your servant. It's easy when I feel happy, rested, relaxed. Do you have something to tell me?

–*Only in my eternity will you see where the torrent ends. The current that moves it is the same as the one you'll discover after death. There will be no more snags or rocks. You won't feel like clinging to the bank.*

April 21 (the chapel)

Eucharist—Gospel: The shepherd leads his sheep to graze in green pastures.

We speak to each other:

–It doesn't seem to me that your pastures are always so delicate, green, or agreeable.

–*You're not a sheep. Stop looking at things at ground level.*

One evening, at Eucharist in the chapel, I speak to him:

–You're not going to visit me any longer. It's already more than a year that we have been meeting. But it's going to come to an end, isn't it?

–*Nicole, I have already spoken to you so often, given you so much. Now it's time to put into practice what I've told you.*

–I'll try.

The next day:

–*I've really spoiled you.*

It's true, I know it. An image of jewelry – pearls – comes to me. The jewelry is lustrous and I'm intrigued by it.

–*The jewelry represents my words to you. These necklaces and all this finery are what you have received and what in some sense you have worn. But now, Nicole, you have to wear this jewelry on the inside. Do you understand?*

–Yes.

But I know I'm going to need time.

May 13 (the chapel)

Gospel of Saint John.

So much love overwhelms me. I glimpse something like a powerful and infinite current binding the Father to the Son.

–Thank you, Jesus, for having chosen us as your friends. Thank you for having allowed us to enter this privileged circle.

–*You are not inside the circle. You haven't been invited into some kind of club. That isn't it at all. You take part in the very movement.*

–What do you mean?

He gives me the image of a triangle. The three corners are bound together by a perpetual movement going from one corner to the other. Each of the poles acting as a point of attraction, drawing the force of the movement. We are in the force itself. We are not on the outside or on the inside of the triangle, but a part of the force of the movement itself.

1986 (vacation)

For a few months now Jesus seems not so much distant as silent. After a year of dialogue that was both marvelous and disconcerting, am I now going to enter into the night?

With a smile on his face, the only thing the Lord said to me was:

—Assimilate this little notebook, this treasure that I've given you.

—As you wish, Lord. I'm going to try . . . and to let go.

9
0

Come and Dance
with Me

July 1986 (vacation in Greece with Philippe and the children)

We backpack from island to island, happy to be to-gether even if once in a while we get on each other's nerves. We each have our own likes and dislikes, and so we have to try to compromise. In this vacation setting where the sky is blue – a strangely limpid blue – and the sea lovely and gentle, it's difficult, almost impossi-ble, to encounter him. I feel bad and tell him so.

–I'm getting you ready. Don't worry about anything.

But still I feel like something of an orphan. I espe-cially feel like a stranger among this hoard of scruffy tourists who are only interested in buying things. It's such a pagan world!

But at Patmos, in the cave where Saint John wrote the Apocalypse, I was finally able to find you, Lord. All

by myself, eyed by a Greek Orthodox priest who was afraid I was going to steal one of the golden treasures that filled the poor grotto, I knelt and wept. The certainty that Jesus is living flooded me. My tears were my only prayer. Saint John should understand.

August (back at the Community)

The Community has gotten bigger with the arrival of a hermit looking for the horizontal dimension of the cross, namely, contact and interaction with the poor, and of a chaplain from a psychiatric hospital who spends a week of his vacation with us cleaning beans and helping with the scrap iron and old paper. *Sharing* is a difficult word for me. But when I saw you in your work clothes, Father Simon, becoming little in the midst of these little ones, I was able to see what sharing means.

In our two poor and barren chapels, three priests celebrate the Eucharist every day. We are being spoiled. I find strength and comfort in the breaking of the bread. Without him, we wouldn't be here. The mission we have been entrusted with is crazy, impossible. How can we possibly help these men? All we can do is be present to them with the love that Jesus has bestowed on us. As for human solutions, we have little, very little, to offer. We don't have the time or the help to make new men out of them. Whether they're alcoholics or psychologically disturbed, at some time in the future they're going to go back to their old ways. All we are is a tiny speck of light. A little bit of a candle that lights up their night. It's so little, but it can really be a lot if Jesus wants to make a bigger light out of it. That's his part. Our part is being satisfied with being tiny little specks of light.

August (chapel of the Companions)

–*Believe in me. Believe in me, all of you.*

–You're very insistent.

–*If you believe in me, you give me impetus. I need your faith in order to act. The drive comes from you.*

August (the chapel)

–*I am master of the impossible. Do you believe that?*

–Yes.

My yes is a little timid, because I don't really believe it. I say "yes" with an obedient mind, but the rest of me says "maybe."

–*You don't understand. It's my impossible, not yours.*

–Hmm! . . . That sounds like a bit of a pirouette, doesn't it?

–*No. My impossible will amaze you.*

August (on the road to the Community)

–I'm amazed by what you do for me, with me, for them.

–*Keep on being amazed. Keep on.*

August (mass at the Companions)

The Gospel about the foolish and prudent virgins.

In silence we meditate on this Gospel.

–Jesus, am I one of the foolish or one of the prudent? Is my lamp full of oil?

–*Only half full.*

–*Oh la la.* . . . What do I have to do, Lord?

–*Nothing.*

–What do you mean? I don't understand and that worries me.

–*Don't worry. Don't worry about anything. It is I who will fill your lamp.*

–Oh! . . .

I promise myself to ask him how tomorrow. But first I have to make what he's telling me my own.

August (the next day, at mass)

I'm a bit apprehensive as I ask him after the Consecration:

–Are you going to explain it to me?

–*Yes.*

–Tell me.

–*You fill the first part of your lamp. I'll fill the second part, and I'll even fill it to overflowing.*

–!!

–*Believe in me. I am your friend. I'll protect you. All you have to do is believe from the bottom of your heart, and your lamp will be filled.*

–You want me to do that, come what may?

–*Yes.*

–It's not that easy, you know.

–*It's much easier than you think. Let go. Don't let anyone make you doubt. Look at everything I'm giving you. Isn't that enough?*

–Oh yes, but . . .

–*Get rid of that "but."*

September 1 (the chapel of the Companions)

The hermit who has been with us for two months is leaving. This is his last mass at the Companions. I en-

trust him to the Lord. He knows what thoughts are up-setting me and the sadness that weighs down my soul.

Jesus comes and gently kneels in front of me and takes me in his arms. It's wonderfully comforting.

–*Believe in me. I won't abandon you.*

And then:

–*Love without any security.*

–I have the impression that all our efforts to draw people out of their misery, to draw them to you, are coming to naught.

Intellectually I know that we're doing the right thing, that we have to love those who are down and out, but sometimes it's difficult to put it into practice.

Jesus adds:

–*I'll continue to spoil you. Don't be afraid.*

September 2 (at home)

In fact, he was not going to put off spoiling me, because the next day, out of the blue, a friend came to the house to ask if Jean-Jacques, a Franciscan priest who lives in the streets with the homeless, could celebrate mass at our home. Of course he could!

Jean-Jacques came. He's gotten very thin and his face is emaciated. My kids are captivated, and the few members from the lay community "Companions of the Lamb" who are also present are fascinated by him. At the Consecration the Lord comes face to face with me.

–*I told you, didn't I?*

Jean-Jacques gives us an hour-long teaching. I dare-say he really doesn't teach me anything. I already know it. In his own way, Jesus has already made me know it inwardly. What Jean-Jacques brings is a flash of light-ning, strong and intense. What authority this man of

God has. I'd love to share my little notebook with him. Someday perhaps.

September 3 (Companions)

Since Pierre left to preach a retreat, everything has become more difficult. The men don't like to take orders from a woman. One of the volunteers wants to be in charge but does everything wrong. I find out that some of the Companions at the Hermitage have been drinking. I'm going to have to come down hard on them. This morning I need to remind them that none of them is to consider himself a little boss.

So here I am, once again becoming tough and blunt. But that's the way it has to be. If I don't take charge, there will soon be chaos.

—*Love them. Even as you do what you have to do, love them.*

It's not easy, and today, with all these proposals and activities happening at cross-purposes, I've had it.

—*Love them. They're weak, often incompetent, and they lie. Love them. That's how they are, the people I am lending you.*

September 4

On the way to the Hermitage, I speak to him.

—Lord, I'm going to have a meeting with them, and I'm going to have to bawl them out because of this damn alcohol.

—*Bawl them out and love them at the same time.*

I don't think any more about what I'm going to tell them. I let myself be soothed by the sight of fields in sunlight. I love the Beauce.

The meeting: they're here and they look ill at ease. I'd like to tell them that I love them, but that's impossible. It just wouldn't work. But I say it in other words. In brief, I tell them that everyone does stupid things, including me. What you have done is pretty stupid. Admit it and let's get on with it.

The principal culprit leaves on his own without my having to ask him. He's not going to make it by himself. I tell him so and affirm my affection for him. Pierre does, too.

–I know, he tells me.

The Lord made everything easy for me because deep down I'm at peace. Today, at that very moment, I was purified of all judgment about them.

Four of us are at the eucharistic service, and I thank him.

–*What did I tell you? Go forward. Follow me. It's easy. Nothing will happen to you.*

September 5 (the chapel of the Companions)

I was afraid that I was going to be all alone in the chapel, but nothing of the sort. Jean-Jacques returned with his little Franciscan brother. At the moment of the Consecration I'm violently dragged back over the centuries. The hands that raise the host and that take and offer the wine are those of Christ. It's brutally intense, inescapable. The gestures, the words: *it's happening for the first time*. Today, at this moment, I'm in the chapel, and *at the same time* I'm present at the Last Supper. This isn't a repetition, a "re-something." This is the real thing, the first time. With my whole being I'm present at the first meal when Jesus shared his own body and blood.

It's crazy. It's like being drunk. Dare I say that I'm "soused"? It's such a vulgar word, but that's more or less what I experience, what's granted to me.

I had no part in bringing this about. I don't deserve all these graces. I don't have words to express what's happening. What comes back to me in my heart are the words of Jesus: *"I will make you a queen."*

September 6

A rich, exhausting, chopped-up day. Divided between the two locations of the Companions, the Hermitage and the Rue des Comtesses. Part of the day is taken up with a group of German friends and benefactors whom we welcome and show around. Uncle Pierre, a monk of Saint-Benoît-sur-Loire, stops in and brightens my day. I'm living in the present, moment by moment. Things are moving fast, but I promised myself that I wouldn't go into a skid or get frazzled. One thing at a time; one person at a time. By this I mean that when a Companion or someone else is talking to me, I try to focus on that person. I don't always succeed, but I'm working on it.

The little chapel is full: two Companions and some friends of the Franciscans. And here I was afraid I'd be all alone!

Jesus comes and wraps us in his tenderness, happy to see us happy.

—Thank you. You know, I can't help feeling a little scared when I'm all by myself at the head of this flock.

—*I know. Surrender yourself.*

—Why do you insist on that so much? Because you are all-powerful and can do everything?

—*No. I need your faith. I need you to believe in me and to love me.*

–I can't believe that you need my love.

–Yes, I do. I need it to be able to act in you and through you. Do you understand?

–What you want is a relationship?

–I am alive.

Weekend at home

Benoît and I were talking about religion, faith, the mass, etc.

–What it comes down to, says Benoît, is a kind of Socratic method that the Lord uses to guide your imagination.

–Why do you say that?

–Because you don't hear a voice, like you hear mine, for example.

–Not exactly, but it's something distinct. He really does speak to me.

–Don't get upset, Mom. I believe you.

Saturday at the chapel

Uncle Pierre is celebrating the mass in our little chapel this morning.

I thank the Lord for being here. This time I see the image of a huge carpet being unrolled. The Lord is weaving it, and the threads intertwine. Our encounters, our lives, are the threads and the knots of the carpet. The Lord is the master of it: he does the weaving.

Mass at home, Jean-Jacques and several friends

–Carry me with you. Take me with you. I don't take up a lot of space. Don't weigh yourselves down with anything else but me.

The chapel of the Companions

There are two of us, kneeling before the Lord and reading the Gospel of the day: the centurion who asks the Lord to cure the slave he loves.

–Why this expression of admiration, Lord? Why? You know what's in our hearts. Why do you admire the faith of this centurion?

–*Because he really believes in me. His faith is rooted in his own life. He understands that his life is my gift, and he really believes in me.*

–And you're so deeply touched by that?

–*Yes. He really loves me.*

–But why the intermediaries? Why send friends? But I don't have time now. I have to leave the chapel in order to see the Companions and then get dinner ready. We'll see each other tomorrow, Lord, and then you'll clear it up for me.

On the way to Arcueil and the food bank where I'm supposed to meet Bernard, a brother and friend.

It's raining. I have to maneuver my way around some oversized trucks. I hear:

–*I'll send you along other roads, the way I'm doing now.*

–What an idea, Lord! I'm not a very good driver. Just where is it you want to send me?

–*On the highway of people's hearts. And besides, I'm the one who will do the driving.*

I can already hear Philippe: God knows what he's doing when he doesn't let you get behind the wheel. You're not the queen of the road.

Bernard continues to be faithful to his commitment, in spite of all the work and problems that are piled on him. He, too, is in charge of a community like ours, but he's always available.

Father Jean is here, and so it's possible for us to celebrate the Eucharist. Bernard is at my side, and when he prays he's like a child in God's presence. The Lord must delight in him. We sit down to a meal and good conversation, during which I learn that the food bank is opening many branches. On my way home the Lord begins the conversation.

–*Bernard is a good centurion.*

–Are you continuing yesterday's conversation, Lord?

–*Yes. He's a good centurion. He too makes use of intermediaries.*

–Ah. . . .

Let's go back a little. When I got to the food bank, Bernard and Father Jean were troubled. A man in Bernard's Community was refusing to leave. He was having mystical hallucinations, upsetting the Community, and so on. As I listened to the two of them, it seemed like I was back in the Community of the Companions. It's a familiar story. Anyway, this difficult person shows up at mass. We pray and share together. The poor fellow isn't doing very well. During mass I ask the Lord to take care of him.

And then a little miracle happened, the kind that happens here. Without any effort at all, Father Jean was able to get through to him, and he decided to leave.

Ouf! Bernard calmly explained to me:

–When we have a difficult situation to resolve, I fast and pray. This morning I didn't have any breakfast. For me, that's a real sacrifice.

Little brother Bernard, good centurion, you amaze me!

–Was fasting Bernard's intermediary? The friends of the centurion sent him to you. Is this case similar?

–*Yes. The intermediaries make it possible for me to weave my fabric along with you.*

Mass at the chapel of the Companions

Gospel: Mary Magdalene pours perfume on the feet of Jesus and weeps.

–*You see, Nicole, she also makes use of intermediaries.*

–The perfume and her weeping, right?

–*Yes.*

I allow a moment of silence to come over me, and I understand that the Lord wants us to use what he gives us – what he gives me – to go toward him. We have to start from what and who we are, not from some external system. The intermediaries are within our reach.

Mass at the chapel

–*Love me. Allow me to love you. Let me act in you.*

Later:

–*Love me starting with your own life, starting with everything I give you to be and to live.*

Mass at Saint Aignan

–*I will make you a queen. Remain little. Have a smile on your face. Be joyful.*

His tenderness floods over me.

Mass at the chapel

–*Be innocent. Remain innocent.*

–But that's so hard, Lord. It's because of you that I have come to recognize and experience all this human misery. You want us to be innocent in the midst of all this?

–*Listen, accept, sympathize, but don't allow yourself to be worn down. Keep on being innocent with me, new with me. Leave the initiative to me, as well as the carrying and*

the doing. Don't be afraid. Be innocent and accept every-
thing and everyone. I'll do what needs to be done.

September 23 (on the way to the Community)

Once more I'm intensely happy to be alive and to be so
in touch with the world and especially with Jesus. The
world in which we live is prey to violence. I have a
friend who is very sick; I'm assailed by all sorts of petty
administrative problems. And yet I feel such a sense of
harmony within myself as I make my way to the Community. The street is as ugly as ever, the human and or-
ganizational problems that I'll have to take care of in a
little while are no joke, and still I feel like singing. What
a gift that is.

I say to him:

—I'm really spoiled, Lord, and I really sense that you
take delight in me. But what about the others, Jesus?
Why do they have less than I?

—What do you know about that?

—Take Philippe, for example, and others as well. I'm
blessed with this intense dialogue with you that so
many of your other friends would like to have. There
are priests, sisters, many others . . .

*—Nicole, you're looking at the back of the tapestry that I
am weaving along with you. I see it from the front. When
you're with me, you'll see it as I do: from the front.*

—I have no desire to die right now. Not at all! Not at
all!

He smiles and continues:

*—Do you see? It's like a painting or a picture. A large
block of brilliant color needs a little dot, a tiny little speck
alongside it in order to make the color come alive. If that
luminous little dot is missing, the block of brilliant color
won't shimmer. Do you understand?*

–Yes. But I have the impression, Lord, that I'm nothing but a big red brush stroke.

–*That could be. Make this stroke shimmer. Make it shine out.*

And then he continues:

–*Be content with seeing only the back of the tapestry. It's a bit of a mess. There are threads all over, tangled colors, and parts left unfinished. But all these overlapping pieces, this jumble, produce the impression of unity and harmony from the front. Do you understand?*

–Yes, Lord. I'll be patient.

Mass at the chapel

There are four of us. I feel a little distant. I need to be silent. Suddenly I'm invaded by a sense of peace, but it's so strange, like a fierce, heavy weight that crashes down on me. I feel completely immersed, out of touch, buried and yet present. What an expression of love!

–Why such great love, Lord? Why me?

–*Because I love you. It's free.*

I have the impression that every part of me is bathed in an incredible tenderness. It's almost too much. I tell him so.

–*Really, Nicole? Why do you not simply accept the gracious gift of my love?*

–Because, because . . . I'd like to give you something in return. We're not equals. I don't deserve it. . . .

I realize that I'm getting all mixed up, and then suddenly everything becomes clear.

–*Be little,* he tells me.

Yes, everything becomes clear. We're not talking about becoming little by willing to be so, by obedience, by a decision. No. This is a littleness that comes about

as a *result* of something else. God's love, God's outrageous love results in our becoming little because we can't act or be otherwise.

Something inside me used to rebel when I was told that we don't amount to much or that we are good for nothing. Deep down, I know I am precious in God's sight, and in the sight of others as well. I'm worth something, and I refuse to say I am nothing. I should say, I used to refuse. Because all of a sudden and deep inside I understand perfectly that *being little isn't something negative*. It's not a matter of diminishing oneself, making oneself small so that the other can have the most space. No, Jesus *already* has an immense space, and all I have is a little space. But *the little space I have is marvelous*. I'm not put down, diminished. I'm simply overcome by the love that I feel in this moment, and I can only declare that he inhabits everything, includes everything, penetrates everything.

And so I'm not going to try to compete. In the face of so much, I yield with joy.

–I really do want to be little in this way, Lord. I really do, because when I do, I feel like a queen.

–*Nicole, if you knew just how intense my love is, you'd be paralyzed. You wouldn't be able to move.*

–I believe you, Jesus. I believe you.

It really is from the inside that he allows me to enter into his kingdom. It's mad. I begin to cry. It's stronger than I am.

September 25 (the chapel)

–Gather me into yourself, Lord, because I'm not managing to place myself in your presence.

–*I will gather you in.*

I feel hopelessly scattered. My mind doesn't obey me and goes wandering off in all directions. This evening's dinner, Laurette's homework, tomorrow's shopping. . . . If I keep on this way, he won't come. So I try as hard as I can to quiet down. *Ouf!* At the Consecration I'm finally more ready to receive him.

–It would be stupid to miss a meeting with you, Lord.

He doesn't reply.

After the Consecration, I finally have some peace and quiet.

–Thank you.

–Keep your eyes wide open to the world, to the events and people that I place in your life. But keep your eyes closed when you're on the way. I will lead you on the way. Don't worry. Be like a child and let yourself be led.

I need to look inward, to listen to his word and follow his road.

September 26

Ever since this morning the idea has been running through my head that the Lord is a "marginal." As I'm doing housework and preparing lunch, I wonder if it comes from him or from me. I'll wait. Maybe this evening at mass.

Mass at the Hermitage.

The Gospel: "Who do you say that I am?"

–You're the "marginal," Jesus? Is that it?

–Yes.

–Explain that a bit. Does it mean you're out on the fringe?

–Yes. Don't try to close me up in a system, file me in a drawer. I'll spill out of the drawer. Don't try to contain me,

*to bring me down to size. If you do that, I'll escape from you.
Do you understand?*

—Yes, I understand. But then how do we reach you,
learn from you, meet you?

—*Heart-to-heart, Nicole.*

—Yes, I think I know that. Is there any other way?

—*No.*

—Well then, what a responsibility, this dialogue, this
heart-to-heart talk with you. What an opportunity! But
looking at it this way is a little scary, Jesus.

—*Don't worry, Nicole. We are two.*

September 27 *(the chapel of the Companions)*

—*I am inviting you. I myself am inviting you.*

September 28 *(mass at the chapel)*

A hectic day. We are beleaguered by telephone calls, er-
rands, and a trip to the Hermitage and back. Pierre
seems drained this evening. My heart aches as I see him
sitting at the table in the chapel. There are three of us.

After the Consecration the Lord says to me:

—*Come and dance with me, Nicole. Come.*

This is too much! Too much! I feel a few moments
of panic as I hear a little voice inside me say, "You're
mistaken. Your imagination is playing tricks on
you. . . ."

I burrow down into the silence.

—Come and help me, Lord. Is it you who are speaking to me?

—*Come and dance with me. Come. I am inviting you.
Don't leave me by myself.*

At that I explode.

–Look here, Lord. You're going too far. Don't you think this is a bit much? The world is in a mess, Pierre is physically exhausted, the Companion next to him tonight isn't any better. And you're asking me to dance with you?

I'm screaming inside.

–Yes. Come.

A few minutes of silence pass. He's sad.

–Come. Don't leave me by myself. I'm not asking you to come and dance with the world, but with me.

–You want me to come and enjoy being with you?

–Yes.

–And all the rest, all the others? All that comes later?

–Yes.

And that's how Jesus inwardly leads me to discover praise and joy. It's really crazy.

September 29 (mass at the chapel of the Companions)

Always this nagging fear that he won't come. There are four of us this evening. During the mass, before the Consecration, he speaks to me gently, as if to reassure me.

–I'm like a raincoat.

–What a strange notion, Lord.

But I wait. If this is really from him, he will explain it to me.

After the Consecration:

–You put me on like a raincoat.

–Go on.

–I am the raincoat. You feel me. The lining is pleasant to the touch. The storms, the wind, the rain will come and drench the raincoat, but not you. Do you understand? I protect you.

–The wind, the storms, the rain . . . all these are our human and material difficulties?

–*Yes. I don't take them away. I protect you. First* live *in me.*

September 30 (at the chapel)

Gospel: Luke, the end of chapter 9.

–I'm following you, Jesus. We are following you. But the plow is hard to manage.

–*You're mistaken.*

–Ah. . . .

–*Yes, you're mistaken. I am the one who opens the furrow, who moves ahead. The plow is me.*

–What about me? What about us? The plow can't go forward all by itself.

–*Take hold of it. Grasp it with both hands. If you hold it steady and do your best to guide it, I'll do the rest.*

10

I Am Not a Moralist

October 3, 1986 (the Hermitage)

I have just made the rounds of the farm. The Companions are working. There is a kind of peacefulness. And yet these are broken men. I stop in the chapel for a few moments.

–Thank you for this peace, Lord. Every time I come out here, I'm just amazed how well these men are able to live together.

–*They are the image of what you are for me.*

–Do you mean that sometimes, like them, we are miserable and unfaithful, and then, at other times, gentle and obedient?

–*Yes. Treat them as I treat you. Be patient, watchful. If they decide to leave you, to abandon what you hold out to them, love them in spite of everything. Even from afar, continue to love them.*

–Yes, I understand.

And then, after a moment of silence:

–Lord, is it pride if I say that I'm not like them? Am I being proud? Tell me.

–*You're different, because I dwell in you, I live in you. You're rich because of me.*

As I leave the chapel, I realize that the Lord didn't exactly answer my question. I'll ask him about it tomorrow, or the day after. Later.

October 5 (mass at Saint Aignan)

I speak to him at the beginning of the mass.

–Are you going to answer me, Lord? Clarify some things for me?

–*Yes. Wait.*

I wait. The Gospel reminds us that we are worthless servants.

–Worthless? That "worthless" irritates me. Is it pride?

–*Be like a leaf in the wind, the cold and dry north wind. In autumn the leaf lets itself be carried wherever the breeze takes it. Do you understand?*

–Yes, I think so. You are the wind, and you want me to hand myself over to you completely.

–*Yes.*

And then, once again, everything becomes clear to me.

–My pride consists in not accepting your love simply and totally. That's the way I see it.

–*Yes, Nicole, yes.*

–You really do want me to be like a leaf?

–*Yes.*

–And just like that I'll become worthless, but it doesn't matter. Is that what you're trying to tell me?

–*Yes. What's important is the wind, the immensity of my love.*

What Jesus offers us is an abyss, and in this abyss there is only "life to the full." And all I can do is hem and haw and protest that "it's too good to be true."

At the end of mass I ask his pardon.

–You talk to me, you give me proof upon proof of your love, and still I hesitate.

He smiles. He seems happy to have cleared things up for me.

On my way home I tell myself that Jesus really has chosen me. Someday I'll be able to tell him in all sincerity: do with me what you will. I'm going to try, I'm going to make a start. But it makes my head swim.

–I'm going to try. Both of us are going to try, Lord.

October 6 (mass at the Companions)

The Lord comes and invites me and the rest of us to dance.

–Is it because I like dancing so much that you're inviting me again?

–*Yes.*

He smiles. I let myself be led by him, and I'm happy, profoundly happy.

–Do you have something to say to me?

–*Yes. Remove the useless garments you cover me with.*

We continue to dance. He *really* did invite me.

–Just what do you mean?

–*I am neither a moralist nor a philosopher. Rid me of all that. My only garment is tenderness and mercy. Do you understand?*

–Is that why you invite me to dance with you?

–*Yes. I want you to feel this tenderness.*

–You know, I'm so happy when I'm with you that I want it to last.

He smiles.

–*Don't worry.*

October 7

And the dance goes on. We continue to dance, and Mary looks at us, smiling.

–Dance with my Son. It makes me happy.

We go faster. We *really* are dancing! Mary is happy, and so am I, because I love to dance.

Mary says:

–If your head starts spinning as you're whirling around, hold on to him. He will steady you. You won't fall.

Interiorly I *really* am dancing with him.

October 8

I have just been at a dinner with the volunteers who help with the sale of used goods. I'm a little down. Since they're not part of the Community, they don't always take our point of view into consideration. When I say "our," I mean Pierre and me and all that we're trying to do. I know this is inevitable even though there is goodwill on both sides.

–Lord, it's stupid to get upset over such little things. We're all walking toward you and working for you. Why aren't we more united?

–*Nicole, is my invisible kingdom being woven?*

–Yes.

–*Well then?*

–But why don't we have the unity and harmony that

I can feel with others: Bernard, Jean-Jacques, Pierre, Antoine . . . ?

—*Once again, you're mistaken. I am the unity and harmony you seek. If you want to find it, don't look anywhere else but in me.*

—But, Lord, what about those I have just mentioned?

—*They live in me, and you also live in me. Do you understand?*

—Yes.

The Lord is stubborn. He really wants me to dance with him.

October 8 (evening mass at Bon Secours)

There are two of us. In a true spirit of harmony.

—Do you really want me to follow you as if you were living?

—*Yes. I am alive.*

—Where do you want to take me?

—*That isn't your concern. Follow me.*

—All right.

October 10 (mass at the Hermitage)

—*Follow me. Follow me. Come and dance with me.*

—You really are determined to seduce us, Lord.

—*I can deceive your body, and I can deceive your mind, but I can't deceive your heart. Come and dance with me, heart-to-heart.*

October 11 (at home)

I'm doing the ironing and the results are hardly impeccable. In a way, my ironing is an image of what I know

how to do, which is to say, I don't know how to do anything very well. I take that back. When I think about it, it seems to me that I do know how to do two things well: teach or give talks, and knit. The rest falls pretty short. And still the Lord comes to speak to me, to dwell in me, and to lead me into the unknown! It doesn't make any sense. I tell him so.

–Why me? Why are you weaving this adventure between the two of us? Why? Why? Tell me.

–*Because I have chosen you. Because I need you.*

–To go where?

–*Into the unknown. There you have it. Do you accept?*

In the laundry as I continue my so-so job of ironing, I let these words sink into me.

I really should be afraid; at least some part of me should be afraid. Suddenly I feel close to those who betrayed Jesus. Often, very often – in fact, ever since I was a child – I have wondered why the disciples of Jesus who saw his miracles, who lived with him, who saw him walk on the water and multiply the loaves, were so thickheaded, so hardhearted. All those proofs took place right in front of their eyes, and yet. . . . Jesus has given me the incredible gift of speaking to me, of making me grow. And yet, in spite of all these proofs, I quibble. . . .

–*Come and follow me.*

–I'll try. But you're going to have to help me. A lot.

–*I will.*

October 12

A telephone call this morning. Pierre informs me that a Companion has just attempted suicide. They're trying to revive him at the hospital. I'm not completely sur-

prised. We talked yesterday, and in the afternoon especially, when he phoned me, he sounded so miserable
that I suggested he return to the Hermitage. He did. We
weren't there, and he swallowed a bottle of pills.

Philippe consoles me, telling me that this is no time
for "what ifs."

Later, in spite of the sadness I feel – or, rather, along
with it – a sense of peace comes over me. I didn't ask
for it. It's simply given. This evening at mass there is still
no news of the Companion. I speak to him:

–It's you who gives me this peace, Lord.

–*Yes. I am the raincoat. Come and dance with me.*

–This is almost scandalous, Lord. You ask me to
dance with you while a Companion is in the hospital.

–*Come and dance.*

I have my head in my hands, and at the same time I
feel some force drawing my face upwards with great
tenderness. I can't resist. I'm happy.

–Why, Lord? Why this peace?

–*I come first, and then the Companion.*

October 16

A getaway with Philippe for several days in Tunisia.

I alight on another planet, totally different from that
of the Companions. Once again I feel very much the
stranger.

I often distance myself from the group in order to be
alone and to enjoy the sea and the sky.

We speak to each other.

–Lord, now that I have these incredible conversations with you, why don't you come and sit alongside
me? Why don't you just stay with me a little?

–*Later, Nicole. Later, in my eternity.*

I don't give up.

–But why not now? You know that I'd really like to have you stay at my side. I love the way you speak to me. So you could also stay with me and tell me where you're taking me, what you want of me. Then it would be clear and I'd go.

–*No.*

–Why not?

–*I am not an officer, nor are you a soldier. I won't give you orders.*

–I'd almost prefer that you did.

–*I know.*

I let these words sink deeply into me.

–It's really a *relationship* that you want. That's the whole thing.

–*Nicole, I am* alive.

October 20 (the Community)

Back with the Companions again. All sorts of little problems and tensions. Another suicide attempt, and here I am once again in the middle of this "bazaar" where everything happens so fast. Pierre is exhausted but still smiling. There are thirty of us, and besides that during the day Pierre takes care of the street people, giving them a meal in exchange for a little work around the place.

I feel faint.

–We are going to go under, Lord.

–*No.*

Later at mass, after the Eucharist. An image of a slope in the mountains. The Lord is walking in front of us.

–You look like Philippe, Lord.

–*Yes.*

In the mountains, walking behind Philippe, I know that nothing will happen to me. He's a lot stronger than I, and his slow, surefooted stride gives me confidence.

–What is it you want me to understand?

–I'm clearing the way so that it won't be so difficult for you. Let me go well in front of you.

–If it becomes too difficult, will you hoist me up?

–Yes.

October 21

We are back at the chapel with Pierre. We have to have a serious conversation with one of the staff who isn't doing his job and who is proving to be a destructive element in the Community.

Pierre prays. I speak to the Lord.

–Lord, what we are about to do isn't easy.

–Yes, I know.

In some part of me I feel at peace. But I also feel tension and uneasiness. That weighs me down.

–I'm not going to take away the uneasiness and the difficulty, Nicole. Bring my peace to it. Let me walk in front of you.

–All right, Lord.

Pierre opens the Bible to two texts dealing with false prophets. Now we are armed for battle.

I feel my heart beating even before I open my mouth during the interview. I say what I have to say as the person responsible for the Community. I'm firm and decisive. I have to be. But at the same time I have compassion for this man who hasn't been on the up-and-up with us and who criticizes us behind our backs.

Everything goes well, or at least as well as can be expected. The falsehood has been unmasked and a certain level of peace has been restored.

The Lord helped me by keeping me from becoming mean and settling my own accounts. Humanly speaking, it would have been perfectly within my right to do so. But since I put his interests ahead of my own, Jesus gave me compassion instead. I had nothing to do with it. It was Jesus.

There will be other difficult times, I'm sure of it. But tonight at mass I thank the Lord. There is a song in my heart. A prayer meeting with a group of sisters. In general, the Lord is really spoiling me, and the Spirit breathes by making use of me. This evening the image is that of a stairway with steps.

I speak to him:

–Lord, I'm exhausted and empty this evening. Moreover, the image I have this evening must come from me because it's really what Pierre and I have gone through today.

–*Tell them about it, Nicole.*

–Do you really want me to tell them?

–*Yes.*

I hesitate a little, because this evening I really would prefer to be carried along by the others, to let Pierre take the lead and simply follow along.

–*Tell them about it.*

I speak. I tell them we don't have to worry about the whole stairway, just single steps. When it's necessary, Jesus will wait on a step with us, will help us get up on the next one, will hoist us up to the third. Our business, our job, is the step. The Lord takes care of the *entire* stairway. We each have our own part to play.

A little flower from the Lord at the close of the prayer meeting: the sisters attest that it really is the Spirit who spoke through this image.

An elderly sister, on leaving, takes my hand and, holding it in hers, says to me like a Mother Superior:

–Don't be troubled. It's the Spirit who is speaking through you.

October 23 (mass at the chapel)

Great repose. I feel very relaxed, and I have the impression of letting myself sink into a luminous black ocean. It's peaceful, and I feel very much present but also drowsy. I seem to be very, very far away, and yet very much with the people who are participating in the Eucharist. When it comes time for the sign of peace, I'm so buried in the Lord that I can hardly lift my head. Pierre appears transformed, like someone else. His face is the same because I recognize him, and yet he looks completely different. I'm not bothered by it; quite the contrary. It's a little as if his face were washed clean of every human trace, becoming more luminous and less clearly delineated. Is this the way we will look in eternity? Maybe.

–Thank you for giving me a taste of all this, Jesus. Thank you.

And later:

–You're giving me strength. I have the impression that we are going to need it. Thank you.

All Saints vacation with the family

In the car that takes me and seven kids to Batz-sur-mer, I thank the Lord for this week of rest ahead of us and

for the little voices chattering behind me. I'm spoiled. The Lord gives me an image, a peculiar image. It's of a container filled to overflowing with mousse, as if someone had overdone the recipe.

–Tell me why you have given me such a peculiar image, Lord.

–*I am the mousse. If you immerse yourself in me, I'll overflow without your having to do anything. Don't do anything. Let go.*

October 28 and 29 (alone in the Batz-sur-mer church)

I meditate on the image of the overflowing mousse.

–You know, Lord, it's hard for me to accept this "don't do anything." I feel like I'm thousands of miles away from you. This immense love of yours that I feel today is boundless. How can your omnipotence need my collaboration? You, the all-powerful; me, not only little, but in a certain sense nothing at all. And there you are, asking me to make the mousse together with you! You have to admit that this isn't just unsuitable. It's preposterous!

–*Yes, I know.*

–You seem a little sad.

–*Yes.*

A few moments later:

–Do you know what, Lord? I really think there's something impossible about the route you propose for your friends. It's not so surprising that more don't follow you.

–*My words have been distorted, Nicole. I already told you that.*

–You know, interiorly I'm beginning to understand your secret. It's all about heart-to-heart. But it's so un-

settling. I have the impression that I'm like an onion and you're taking away layer after layer. What will be left?

—You. At any rate, each time I take a layer away, I clothe you again with my cloak.

I reflect on what he has said. It's true. I'd be untrue to myself if I thought otherwise. Every time I was afraid and gave this fear to the Lord in order to find peace again, *he gave me peace.* All sorts of examples come to mind. True, I often wept, sometimes screamed inside when I stayed with Françoise as she was dying or as I prayed for Jean-Marie.

And you, Lord, you gave me Bernard to trust in me when I was ready to give up. You gave me Cécile's smile and her helping hand when I felt so bad for her. All those for whom and with whom I suffered are with you and me, as if we were welded together. It's true.

And later:

—What do you want me to do?

—Intercede.

—As Thérèse told me to do?

—Yes.

And, in fact, at night, before I go to sleep or when I wake up in the night, I entrust to the Lord the prayer intentions that people have given me.

—Don't worry, Jesus. I'm going to try.

November 1 (mass at the church, Batz-sur-mer)

Our number rose to fifteen two days ago, and this evening, without any argument or bickering, we headed off to church.

The children are here with their friends. They're all different, and some of them hardly ever go to mass, but

they're here. My heart is filled with joy during the mass. Martine, a friend of mine, is next to me. We don't talk, but I know that the three of us are united.

–Thank you for Martine, for the children, for this vacation.

There is something touching about this odd little group. These days have been marked by a heightened sense of peace and joy.

It's hard to forget the young people – or the grown-ups – who are sitting in the two pews behind us. And I can hardly keep from laughing when Benoît, who is taking up the collection, makes a scene and accuses me out loud of putting "Turkish" money in the collection basket. In fact, some Tunisian coins did get into my purse by mistake.

After Communion I try to draw closer to Jesus and to be silent. It's a little tough to do.

–*I will do wonderful things through you.*

A few moments later:

–Are you going to tell me once again to let go?

–*Yes.*

And a little later:

–*Let go. Be light, like a seagull.*

–Light?

–*Yes, light. Don't weigh others down and don't try to control them too much. Be light; not indifferent, but light.*

–Why?

–*Because the lightness allows me to come through. I'll take charge. I'll do the carrying. Your lightness will point to me, will unveil me.*

Back at the chapel

The Lord comes and sits down next to us.

–*Hold on to my hand.*

A little later I have the image of two hands inter-twined. The image is strong. Is it something I have dreamed up? I wait. The confirmation comes from Pierre. "Thank you for being in love with us," he says. After the Consecration, Jesus clarifies its meaning for us:

–*Walk with me. Go forward. Let's go forward like lovers.*
–Please go on. Explain it further.
–*Carefree, both of us lighthearted, like lovers.*

Mass in the chapel, Companions and friends

Today it's difficult, almost painful, for me to immerse myself in the Lord.

–I feel far away from you, Lord.
Silence.
–Such mediocrity today, Lord.
–*Give it to me.*
–Take it, Lord. It seems that's all I have to offer today. It's pretty wretched, isn't it?

I feel unhappy and really miserable.

And then, at the very moment I say these words, I'm invaded by a heavy, brutal peace. I feel myself drawn down to the ground. Around me I hear voices giving thanks for this word. Praise ascends from their hearts while I bury myself in a kind of thick cloud. I seem to be between two worlds. My heart is warmed by the praise.

–Listen, Lord, receive it. They're crying to you.

On the road to the Hermitage

I'm all by myself. And so we talk – or rather, I talk and he listens. My words to him today are terribly common-place, little more than "thank you" and "I love you."

Before arriving at the farm I pass a wooded area. The colors are magnificent, varied, and resplendent. I have the impression that I'm seeing them for the first time.

—*It's like my kingdom, Nicole.*

—Your kingdom?

—*My invisible kingdom. You're just beginning to discover it. It will be just as beautiful and varied.*

11

o

Like Me, Unarmed, Vulnerable, Little

November 7, 1986 (on the way to Rome)

Philippe and Thierry have just left me. I carry their two beautiful smiles with me onto the train platform.

While I was on a mini-retreat at Saint-Benoît-sur-Loire, I got the idea during one of my meditation periods to send my little notebook to a family friend who is close to the pope.

–Go ahead, my uncle Pierre, a monk at Saint-Benoît, said to me. That's not a bad idea at all.

So I sent my notebook to Rome. On the very day of my birthday our friend called to say he would like to meet me. It was ten o'clock in the evening, and it was hard for me to understand him because the connection was so bad. At one point I thought he was one of the Companions and almost got angry with him!

Several days later, at the Apostolic Nuntiature in Paris, I met him and discovered a great man of God. I was struck by his sharp intelligence, by the way he listened, by his love for Mary, and, above all, by his humility. I had been afraid that I was going to meet an ecclesiastical dignitary who would advise me to take care of my children and my husband and to be careful about a certain kind of mysticism. On the contrary, I met a brother. He was attentive, gentle, happy to listen to me. In no time we were at the heart of things: Mary, the pope, the importance of marriage . . . and the question that was most central for me:

—How do you manage to hold the two together?

Sensing my incomprehension, he explains:

—How do you hold together the violent world of the Companions and that of your family?

I tell him. He listens with eyes closed and he understands. He understands everything: what is at stake in keeping a balance, the squabbles, my enthusiasm about continuing because, with Pierre and prayer, I'm armed.

—Continue, he tells me. Like the pope, you are not afraid. Continue.

The hour passes. I have to be on my way. He gives me back my treasure.

—Come to Rome. I'd like the pope to give you his personal blessing. Come whenever you like.

And so here I am on the train for Rome. I didn't plan this. I didn't ask for anything. In my head ring the words of the Lord, *"I will make you a queen."* And at the same time I remember Pierre's advice: "Little servant. Always be a little servant." Both at one and the same time. My head and heart are filled with those who have

led me to this joy. My grandmother, my father who on a day when I experienced a great setback told me to pray to Mary, Uncle Paul, Uncle André, Uncle Pierre . . . and now Bernard and Pierre.

What beacons! How tightly we are bound together! All of you are very much alive and present in my heart, and I'll make time to pray with you and for you.

November 9 (Rome)

I have been invited to mass in my friend's private chapel. There are three of us. It's very simple. Even though I'm in a palace that houses several cardinals, even though I'm far away from the open skies of the Beauce, this chapel is so much like ours that I feel at home. It's small and simple. It's the same family that comes before the Lord.

Before going to sleep I thank the Lord for spoiling me like this. I confide to his care this older brother with whom I have been able to share prayer and daily life so deeply.

–*Stay small,* Jesus says to me the next day.

–Yes, Lord, but you know, I may not be able to keep myself from being proud!

–*Little, Nicole,* little.

–I have you, the Son of God, for my friend. I carry within myself all those you have given me. And the day after tomorrow I'm going to see the pope. How can I help being proud?

–*Proud, but little.*

–Why are you so insistent?

–*So that you'll let me walk well in front of you.*

November 10 and 11 (Rome)

I'm going to see the pope . . . I'm going to see the pope.

That silly little refrain keeps going through my head, taking me back to the times in my childhood when I'd feel like singing a little tune over and over again and dancing to it.

I seem to have become a little girl again, and yet . . . and yet, I feel that there is something that isn't quite right between Jesus and me.

As I go from church to church, I often stop to pray, of course. And each time it seems as if Jesus is repeating the same words to me: *"Be little."*

It's become almost an obsession. In the crowded bus I'm riding, I say to him:

–You're so insistent that it makes me feel uneasy.

He doesn't reply.

So I insist.

–What is it, Jesus? You seem to be sad. Tell me why.

–*Take me along.*

–What? That's a bit strong. It's your home I'm going to.

–*I don't have a home. Take me with you.*

I'm nonplussed. Silence.

–Do you feel hurt?

–*Yes.*

I want to argue with him, to assure him of my good faith, and then suddenly I realize that it would be useless.

In completely good faith, I had quite simply forgotten about him. Like a little child following behind, he had to remind me he was there. It's all topsy-turvy. I'm the one who is taking Jesus with me to see the pope!

I'm totally confused. I wait until I'm calm again before I promise him:

–I'll take you with me. I promise.

November 12 (Rome)

I promised, and so I do it. He's at my side as we enter the audience hall.

Thanks to my friend, I was in the first row and could see the pope close-up. The presence and power of this man are awesome.

–Lord, watch over him, clothe him, dwell in him.

That was practically my only prayer.

When John Paul approached me and looked at me for a few seconds before blessing me, what I saw was the look of a man who has been, is being, crucified. Yes, this man has already been crucified. I was literally swallowed up by his gaze, a look so deep it seemed to come from some faraway place and to be filled with a tenderness that was forceful and direct.

Carry on, Father. Even though you may be all alone and everyone is against you, carry on.

There is such solitude about this man.

I prayed for this man, John Paul II, asking Jesus to come and dwell in his solitude.

November 13 (Rome)

A day of shopping in Rome.

Yesterday's joy fills my day.

Friday, November 14 (Rome)

Last night and all day today were tumultuous. I feel as if I'd been in a knockdown, drag-out fight. There's no other way to describe it.

Every morning I have been getting up early to go to mass. Up till now I always experienced the same feeling

of joy that I feel when I go to mass at the Companions. But this morning I was overtaken by a feeling of heaviness. There is no reason for it. During the mass I know the joy of the encounter, but at the same time I feel such a heavy weight that tears stream from my eyes. I can't do anything to stop them, these tears of sadness. The feeling lasts all morning long and I have to ask myself some questions. This isn't normal because there is absolutely no reason to be sad. Quite the contrary. Everything makes me happy for one reason or another: all that I'm experiencing here, the people I carry in my heart, the freedom of time and space that has been afforded me. And yet . . .

Exhausted from struggling against tears whose origin I don't know but that I can hardly contain in the presence of others, I retire to my room and let them flow. They pour out. I feel completely despondent.

I'm going to try to rest and get some sleep, but before I do that, I speak to him.

–Lord, I don't understand anything, and that makes it so hard. If I knew why, or perhaps if I knew what to call this unknown depression, I could deal with it. But I don't know.

No reply.

–All right. I place my heart next to yours. Protect me, because I'm weak and ignorant. If it's the evil one that has been troubling me, protect me.

I cry myself to sleep.

I wake up an hour later. The tempest has passed. I feel lighter.

After calmly taking the time to write some letters and cards, I go down to the chapel.

–It's better now, Lord. But I really don't understand what happened to me.

—You have passed through a little bit of the night; you have carried a part of my cross.

—Is it you, *you, Jesus,* who are sending me this?

—Nicole, Nicole . . .

—But put yourself in my place.

—Nicole, I am shaping you. You have to know, have to experience this part of my kingdom, too.

I allow these words to sink in. This is something new. It's not easy, and I try my best to discern if it's he or my imagination.

Finally I'm able to smile. The little lamp burning next to the tabernacle warms me.

—I'll follow you, Lord. I'll follow you.

—It wasn't so difficult after all, so heavy. Don't you see how near I am?

A little touch of humor on the Lord's part.

November 19 (back home, the little chapel, Eucharist)

It's not easy to place myself in the Lord's presence once again. My head is swimming with images and impressions of Rome and especially of the strength I had the good fortune to draw on. I feel it inside me. It's something that wells up and abides in me.

—Lord, I feel distant and empty, a bit like a foreigner. I don't feel ready. Come.

Silence. Jesus isn't bullied. I can't summon him. There is no call button. He is, and he is gentle, and I flounder around, but I know he's here and very much alive.

—Still, come and speak to me. You know how much I need to hear you. Come.

Silence.

After the Consecration:

–Make some room for me. Your house is too full.

–What do you mean?

–There is too much furniture in the room set aside for me.

–When you say room, do you mean our hearts?

–Yes.

–What do you want us to do?

–Remove what isn't absolutely necessary. Then I'll be more comfortable being with you. Give me lots of space.

–Remove? All right, but what?

–Your cares, your useless worrying. Don't weigh yourself down.

It's not all that easy to put our cares aside. I try. A little later.

–Nicole, I was born in a stable.

In a stable! . . .

November 20 (in town)

For the past couple of days I have been questioning myself and meditating on "detachment." My friend who was so kind to me in Rome spoke about it during one of the masses in his little chapel, and I have been thinking about it ever since. I find it disconcerting. In Rome I had said to the Lord:

–When you like, will you explain it to me?

–Yes.

Today, as I'm walking to the Secours Catholique, he clarifies what it means.

–Once again, Nicole, it's not something negative.

–You're right. Once again I was under the impression that it was something negative . . . that to detach oneself is in some way to love less. But the fact is you give me people to love and who love me.

–Be like the pope.

–Ah! . . . The pope?

–Yes. He has his arms wide open. Be like him.

–That's detachment?

–Yes.

–What do you mean?

–Love, Nicole, love all those I give you. Love. But don't hold them too tight, not one of them alone or all of them.

–Why not?

–If you did, I wouldn't be able to give you anyone else. You wouldn't leave me enough room.

–I understand. Do you have anything else to tell me?

–Yes. If you do this, I will love in you.

–How will you manage that?

–I will inscribe them in your heart. I will love them in you. Not only will I not take them away, I will inscribe them in you. Do you understand?

–Yes.

Oh yes, not only do I understand, but I have been reassured and given a sign of appreciation. *I'll inscribe them in you.* Who am I that Jesus should come and do this in me? Who am I? I am literally flooded with joy. I feel like crying, like shouting thank you, but all I can do is say to him in a low voice:

–Thank you. Thank you. Go ahead. Inscribe them in me.

"Abandon yourself," my brother in Rome had told me. I went away carrying these two words as a child carries her treasures.

And at this very moment, I abandon myself.

November 22

The sweetness of Jesus caressing my cheek after the Eucharist.

–Don't make any plans. I'll take care of everything.

November 23 (chapel, in town)

The Apocalypse of Saint John.

Pierre emphasizes that we are chosen. I'm bothered by the word *irreproachable*.

–Lord, you have chosen us, but I'm far from being irreproachable.

After the Consecration, he gives an explanation:

–*The woman of the Gospel, the one who gives what is essential. Be like her!*

I meditate on this, but I don't get the connection with the word *irreproachable*.

–You want me to give what is essential. You really want the essence of who I am?

–*Yes, everything. The good and the not-so-good. Everything.*

–As to the good, Lord, you know that I'm not stupid, that I've done advanced studies and am a good teacher. Sometimes it's a little difficult to give all that up to take care of thirty guys who come in off the street. Is that the essential that you want?

–*Yes. Your gifts, your intelligence, but also your limitations and your deficiencies. Give me all of it.*

–Jesus, you know that I don't do too badly with the talents you've given me.

–*I'll do even better than you. Don't you believe that I'll be able to do at least as well as you?*

–Of course. But what about the part that's not so good, the limitations, the deficiencies?

–*There I'll do what you're not able to do.*

–You have an answer for everything. You always corner me.

–*No, I don't corner you; I set you on course.*

The Lord isn't any more distant from me, but he shows himself in a different way.

Mass at the Companions

—I'm building a wall to protect you. I myself am this wall, within you and around you.

December 8 (mass at the Companions)

—Take me now as your protector. From the very depths of your being.

December 9 (prayer with the Bon Secours sisters)

It's hard for me to place myself in the presence of the Lord. A little later, I speak to him.

—Make use of me if you need me.

I try to make myself little. Several words rise up in me.

—Let go, Jesus says to me. *Tell them that.*

I don't remember all the words because they didn't come from me. I have a very strong impression that the Lord is speaking to one or the other of the sisters. It's as if I were only a conduit. I feel something inside pushing me to say:

—Go, go to your brothers. Don't try to avoid it. I have put you where you belong.

I feel in my body that these words are meant for someone in the group. I don't try to find out who. That's the Lord's business, not mine.

A little later another phrase comes to me:

—Unarmed, vulnerable, little. That is the way you must go to your brothers. Like me, unarmed, vulnerable, little.

December 10 (mass at the chapel of the Companions)

I have to admit that I'm a little disappointed that I no longer experience the deep interiority of the conversations of the previous months.

–Lord, don't abandon me. I need to hear you.

–*I have already said so much to you, Nicole. Live what I have helped you discover.*

–But I'm afraid.

–*Yes, I know. I can see that.*

Later:

–*Do you really think that I could deceive you? Don't be afraid. Don't doubt.*

December 11 (mass at the chapel)

–*Be lighthearted, carefree.*

–That's a little hard right now, Lord.

–*I want all of you to be lighthearted. Come and throw your arms around my neck like little children. I'll carry you.*

December 11 (mass at the chapel)

–*Be little, abandon yourself.*

–I'm trying to.

–*I'm going to use you like a conduit. Don't get in the way.*

–I'm afraid. What we have to live through is so insane.

–*Don't get in the way. Don't be afraid.*

Later he asks me to say:

–*Don't be afraid. Don't try to make all sorts of preparations for what lies ahead, for tomorrow. I'll give you the strength you need when you need it.*

End of December

The days fly by fast and full. As Christmas draws near I always feel a special kind of joy. This joy is given to

me every year, and I'm happy to go running here and there in search of something that will delight this person or that.

I feel the Lord is watching over me.

Those remarkable moments of intimacy with the Lord haven't disappeared, but they seem to have changed somewhat. During the Eucharist the Lord is close by, certainly, but now I no longer experience moments in which time and space are momentarily suspended. I have to admit that I miss these intense moments, but I'm trying not to make them up or "will" them. There is a deep-down sense of well-being in feeling myself surrounded by the tenderness of God without losing anything of my own personality. It's as if everything I'm searching for, consciously or not, is being realized. What was so fantastic about those moments I experienced was feeling that I was in the arms of Jesus and at the same time closer than ever to those I love. I don't remove myself from them. They're with me *naturally*.

And so how could I not want more of this?

You come when you choose to, is that it? My friend in Rome told me to abandon myself. Pierre often reminds me to be little. So I try.

A day trip to Paray-le-Monial in response to a request from the Sisters of the Cenacle to speak about our involvement with the poor. What a joy it was to see Jeanne's smile again. I spoke to the sisters about the way Jesus takes care of me, of us. I tried to be as sincere and straightforward as possible. Even without trying to be someone I'm not, I find that it's not easy to speak about our life. I have the impression that every time I try to speak or explain what it's all about, I monopolize Jesus or make him into something he isn't. I try to avoid this

kind of distortion by talking from my own life experience. Those who hear me, like those who might happen to read this little notebook, will know what comes from me and what comes from him.

Mass at the chapel of the Companions

—Don't strain. With simplicity accept all that I give you to live. Don't force anything. I'll take care of the rest.

Christmas (Rambouillet, mass)

Whenever I'm in the midst of a gathering that is somewhat agitated and unfamiliar, it's difficult to allow the Lord to enter deeply within me. I tell him so.

—It's difficult, you know, to let go, to come back to you.

—Yes, I know that.

I sense his presence. He's here, alive. He's something like an older brother who wants to let me walk all by myself, but who also wants to protect me. He watches over me. At the Consecration I'm able to say to him in all truth:

—Do with me whatever you wish. I'll be your follower.

I say this with my whole being: head, heart, body.

A little later:

—Lord, I'm being completely honest. You know I am. It wasn't some rush of sentimentality that led me to say what I just said. . . . But I'm not stronger than Saint Peter, you know. You'll have to help me if I should ever leave you.

—Don't worry. I'll come after you and take you by the sleeve.

Christmas Day

The Companions are here, around the table. Pierre is with them. Peace reigns, but hardly anyone speaks. This is a Christmas without wife, without children, without family. I'm absolutely certain that the child who was born in a stable and died on a cross is one of theirs, and that he came for them.

–Lord, I beg you to send out harvesters. Send more Pierres, Bernards, Jean-Jacques. Send even more, if such should be your pleasure.

After Christmas

The rhythm of my life has become rather hectic and broken. The children are on vacation. I have the flu. And then Philippe comes down with it, too. I'm exhausted and have a hard time keeping up. Not feeling the presence of the Lord as strongly as I did a year ago makes me a little sad.

I know that he's here, especially during the Eucharist. I have promised to be little and to abandon myself. So I'll try not to be so sad.

I have the impression that I'm living through a kind of "intermission," both in my soul and also at the Companions. We're letting go.

12

0

My Father Will Come to Visit You

January 10, 1987 (mass at the chapel)

Once again I'm in the presence of the Lord. Pierre, a Companion, Bernadette, and I.

I come before him once again and say:

—As you wish, when you wish. I'm not asking for anything.

A few moments later I'm literally plunged into his presence. It's interminably long and deep. Now I am reassured.

I hear:

—*Little girl, little girl . . . little sister, little sister.*

The words overwhelm me with their tenderness and love. Later I have an image of the Lord walking in front of me like an older brother, while I'm running behind him, trying to catch up.

—Don't be so frantic. Why are you running like that?

—In order to catch up with you.

—Don't be worried. I'll watch over you like an older brother. I'll wait for you. Don't run so fast. Don't force things.

January 11 (mass at the chapel)

—I'm here in your presence. I'm little, as you want me to be.

—Don't worry.

After Communion:

—I am the light. It travels through thick layers of darkness to get to you. You receive only a part of it. That's enough.

The image is very clear to me. It's like the light of a very strong projector that has to cut through thick layers of darkness in order finally to get to us.

—Why all these thick layers, Lord?

—I'll tell you tomorrow.

January 12 (mass in Pierre's office)

It's so cold in the chapel that we have to take refuge in Pierre's office.

Pierre is worn-out, empty. He's been listening to a friend who arrived from abroad and never stopped talking. Pierre is smiling, but I see profound weariness on his face.

Ouf! It's time for mass. Finally we are going to be able to rest with him.

—Lord, there is sorrow in my heart because of Pierre, but here I am, here we all are in your presence. I feel tired, on edge, and short of energy this evening. Come.

I try to submerge myself in his presence and in the rest he offers us.

After Communion:

–What are these thick layers, Lord? You told me you'd say something about that.

–*They're the brutal and violent world that you don't understand. They're unspeakable poverty, the temptation of a Companion to commit suicide last week, Olivier's mental illness, Pierre's sickness. . . . I won't take these things away from you.*

–It would be so simple if you'd explain why these things happen.

–*No. If you were able to understand all that, you'd be a little god. And I don't need one.*

–Then what do you need?

–*Your gift. Yesterday I told you that you've got enough light to rise above these thick layers. In spite of these layers, and with them, give me your love. Leap over them.*

After a few moments of silence:

–Lord, it's a relationship you want, isn't it?

–*Yes.*

There's a certain weariness in this yes.

January 13 (mass at the chapel)

An image, a very strong image, of two points of light that intersect. One of the points, the strong one, is the Lord's; the weaker one is ours. When they intersect, sparks burst forth and then fall.

–*Don't worry about what may result from our encounter. The light and the sparks will come to rest in places you wouldn't imagine. Don't be concerned about it.*

January 14 (mass at the chapel)

From the very beginning of the mass I hear:

–*My love, my love, my child.*

It's overwhelming.

–Give me some sign, any sign, that I'm not imagining these words. Please.

My neighbor reads the text of the day, from the Letter to the Hebrews:

"Therefore, as the Holy Spirit says, 'Today, if you hear his voice, do not harden your hearts as in the rebellion.'"

January 16 and the following days

I have the feeling that I have to put into practice and integrate all that the Lord has revealed to me interiorly, but still I can't restrain myself from telling him how much I miss him. He's not any less present just because I feel him less. No, not that. It's just that our encounters used to be so good and so powerful. He is here, and he is alive. I know that.

–As you wish, when you wish. But if you were to come and visit me as you did before, Lord, that would be wonderful.

Sometimes his only reply was:

–*I have already given you much.*

And:

–*I'm here.*

The other evening, it was different. I was meditating on abandonment, on humility.

–*Enter the room with your head held high.*

–What does that have to do with humility, Lord?

–*Enter my humility as you enter a room, with your shoulders squared and your head held high.*

I think I understand why Jesus tells me that. I refuse to believe (or perhaps I'm not able to believe, I don't know) that humility means bowing and scraping, or at least thinking you should.

–We have to enter into your humility standing up.
–*Yes.*

I don't understand very well what he means by the "room," but he will explain that to me tomorrow.

The next day, at mass with the Companions

–Lord, are you going to explain it to me?

A few moments later I see a room filled with thick haze or with cotton. It's all over the place.

–*Walk toward me; come closer.*

–Are you at the other end of the room?

–*Not only there. I'm also all this stuff that surrounds you. Bury yourself in it.*

–What about humility?

–*That's what humility is, burying yourself in me.*

On several occasions in subsequent days it almost seemed to me that I was being enveloped in this thickness. Two serious problems were confided to me, both of them outside the Community. Once more I became faint in the face of human suffering and my inability to do anything about it. I "literally" buried myself in him as I went to sleep, entrusting to him two people who were all but lost. I felt myself physically enveloped.

Several days later (at the Hermitage)

At mass. I feel myself seized and, as it were, drawn by a point far, far inside me.

–*Bury yourself, bury yourself in me. Go all the way.*

February, March, April

The Lord is silent. Not absent, but silent.

I don't feel like an orphan, nor like one abandoned, but like someone who's waiting.

One evening during a Eucharist in February, I told him that what we were doing in the Community was virtually meaningless.

Reply:

—*It's in this meaninglessness that you resemble me the most.*

If I had the time, I'd have to tell about all the little miracles we experience in the Community. But it takes time to do this, and when evening comes, I feel too drained to write.

We have just spent two weeks without Pierre, and everything went well. Of course, it was necessary to endure, to listen, to knock heads together sometimes, but I felt like I was being "escorted" and, in spite of the weight of these men, "at peace."

December

The misery and distress of some people around me, rich or poor, affects me deeply. Some of them have inherited inhuman situations that they did nothing to deserve. They're so weighed down. It's so unjust. I tell him so.

—What a mess we're in, Jesus. We didn't ask for any of this, we don't deserve it. . . . It's because of sin, Lord, I know. Our sinful condition. But I didn't ask for anything; we didn't ask to be born. I don't feel any solidarity with Eve and her apple, none at all.

I'm filled with anger and revulsion, and also with pain.

Jesus answers me calmly:

—*But I am in solidarity with you, with the others, completely. No matter what the situation, always. Do you understand?*

—I was sure of it, Lord. You always turn everything around.

–No, it's not I who turn things around; it's you.

–What do you mean?

–*You wanted to understand everything, to deal with it on an intellectual level. You talk to me about Eve. You'd like to be the Alpha and the Omega. Once again, you'd like to take the place of my Father.*

His reply immediately calms me down, but I'm not completely satisfied.

–You always answer from the inside.

–*You won't get any other kind of answer. It's from the inside that I fashion my kingdom . . . and you certainly know from experience the marvelous things that can be accomplished even when you have to wallow in filth and mud.*

–Yes, I know, I know. I've been living it for two years, but . . .

–*But don't be in such a hurry. One day in eternity you will know everything.*

I'm not in any hurry, not at all.

Mass at the Carmel

Letter of Paul to the Thessalonians. "Be joyful."

–Here we are again, Lord. Joy, praise, no matter what the circumstances.

The priest expands on the theme, but I'm not at all in agreement.

–What about the tears, what about the suffering that makes the sick cry out in pain? What about children in their hospital beds? What about your agonized cry from the cross, Jesus?

–*I have overcome death, all deaths.*

–But you haven't wiped out suffering. The earth still echoes with the cries of those who suffer. I don't have to tell you. So what about this joy, Lord? What about this joy when Aunt Hélène weeps and is totally worn out

after all those useless chemotherapy treatments? Absolutely not. What the priest is saying is full of lovely sentiment, but it's without flesh and blood; it lacks the real humanity that you yourself have given us. You know that, Lord, you know it better than I.

–*Nicole, it's not your joy we're talking about, but mine.*

–Your joy is different?

–*Of course.*

–What do you mean?

He shows me a piece of fruit.

–Your joy, Lord?

–*It's the pit, the pit of the fruit. Do you understand?*

–Yes. Your joy doesn't necessarily consist in smiles or happiness.

–*No, not necessarily. It's something else, something stronger and more solid. It's the certitude that comes from knowing that I am with you and in you. Do you understand?*

–Yes. This joy doesn't sweep away obstacles.

–*No. It illuminates them from the inside.*

–You always come back to the same point: your kingdom is on the inside.

–*Yes. Were you expecting me to say something else?*

–In the last analysis, your kingdom is utterly "other," "different."

–*Yes.*

–So don't be surprised if so few people follow you, Jesus.

–*I have never looked for the biggest number.*

December (in Chartres)

Christmas is drawing near.

I can never get my Christmas shopping done early; I'm always in a panic as the day draws near. But

it's a time when I feel like a child again and start singing for joy.

Jesus isn't absent, but I have the impression that he's letting me walk on my own two feet. It's as if he were watching over me from a distance, ready to run to my side if I call out. Distant, but not absent.

Christmas, Christmas. . . . With this childlike joy in my heart I feel forty years younger.

January 2, 1988 (the chapel)

Mary's feast day.

    —Be like her, Jesus tells me.

    —You already told me that. You know that I'm trying.

    —Yes, I know.

    —You want me to be ready to give myself, like her?

    —Yes. No looking back. Don't hold on to anything. Neither from the past, nor for the future.

    —Could you tell me what you mean?

    —Don't try to figure things out, don't calculate. Go forward without trying to know what will happen tomorrow or at some future time. Mary didn't say, "Yes, but." Get rid of the "but."

    —It's difficult to give you the unconditional yes you want without understanding what is involved.

    —That is precisely the kind of yes I want from you.

    —You know that's not easy, and besides, I'm afraid. When we follow you, Jesus, the way can become very difficult. I think about Mary and the sword that pierced her heart. When I think of her, I start crying, as you well know, and I begin to feel afraid.

    —Then you don't understand. Look at my cross. I have borne everything. Everything. *And that makes it* simple.

    —Simple?

–Yes. I have taken everything up on my cross. And so, if you're with me, nothing will happen to you.

–Nothing?

–Nothing, provided you include me in everything you do. Provided you give me enough space so that I can be with you. There will be two of us, Nicole. So what can happen to you?

January 3 (the chapel of the Companions)

–Why are you so insistent, Lord. Why do you need this kind of yes?

–So that I can make riches flow from your heart and your hands.

–Is that all! You surprise and amaze me.

–I will make you a queen. I promised you.

–Queen of your kingdom? Of the invisible kingdom?

–Not only that.

–Yes, Lord. Do with me as you will.

January 5 (at the Companions)

Lulu and Chevalier show up at the Community. What a pitiful couple. They're filthy, and they stink. The two of them sleep in an old car. We get a heated trailer ready for them and some clean sheets, but on one condition: they have to take a shower.

Pierre looks at me.

–Okay. I'm going. Come on, Lulu, Chevalier. Let's get in the shower.

With Lulu and me it's the same old melodrama: insult upon insult. To calm her down, I suggest that she go and pick out her own dress and coat. On the way to

the secondhand clothes store, I'm almost overcome by her smell. She never stops yelling at Jim and me as she picks out a dress, refusing a beautiful black coat that I had selected for her.

–It's too dreary, she says. I look better in green.

So much for me!

It's a real circus – the three of us in that tiny shower stall! Chevalier is kind and gentle as he helps me with Lulu. He caresses her lovingly, and that both touches and comforts me. My heart is warmed and things become easier.

Lulu, at last, is clean, calmed down, and finally happy with the change. While Chevalier finishes washing up, she cleans out the sink. She does a good job.

–This place isn't very clean! she says.

My laughter is quickly tempered by the sight of a bottle of wine that seems to have appeared out of nowhere.

–Oh, Lulu!

–A little bit never hurt anybody!

We take away the bottles.

–Not even a little bit to go with the meal? Chevalier complains.

–No.

The time has come to be firm.

The next morning, Chevalier was not in good shape. He and Lulu both had the DTs.

They didn't come back. They had chosen alcohol and couldn't do without it.

I'm disappointed, of course, but at the same time at peace. When I softly caressed Lulu's clean face, she broke out in sobs. Human misery had encountered tenderness and responded with tears.

–Cry, Lulu, my darling, says Chevalier. I love you so much.

That was a piece of eternity for me. The absolutely clear certitude that Jesus loves us unconditionally, in spite of our depravity and our failures.

That evening in the chapel Jesus comes to me and says:

–You see, it's easy; it was simple.

Pentecost

Jesus' silence weighs down on me. I've been spoiled. It's been several weeks now, even months. I try to accept this silence with docility, but it's difficult, and at each Eucharist I can't stop myself from telling him that I miss the sense of his presence.

–As you wish, when you wish, Jesus. But I'd really like to have you come back and speak to me as you did before.

I'm pestering him, I know, but I keep on.

Pentecost Sunday (at Saint Aignan)

Finally he answers me.

–Nicole, I haven't abandoned you.

–No, I know you haven't, but it was better before when we spoke to each other. I miss you, and I'm not going to pretend that it never happened.

–But I'm always here, close to you.

–Not like before.

–No, but it has to be this way.

–Why?

–I only withdrew a little from you to allow you to meditate.

–Meditate on what?

—Your little notebook, my word. It's in the empty spaces, in silence, that you deepen a relationship. You already know that. That's how it is with Philippe.

I'm so reassured I begin to cry.

Monday of Pentecost

A Charismatic Congress at Bourget with fifteen thousand participants. I always feel somewhat lost in such a huge and animated crowd.

He returns.

—Are you reassured now?

—Yes. I needed this.

—I'm not abandoning you. Make an empty space for my presence.

A few moments later:

—Someday I'd like to go on stage and tell people about you. Is that all right with you?

—Yes. There will be a time for that. But don't go too fast.

July 2 (chapel of the Companions)

We buried a Companion the day before yesterday. I can still see his smile when I went to visit him at the hospital, can still feel his hand in mine when we prayed the Our Father and the Hail Mary. After hesitating for a few days, I had asked him:

—Bertrand, would you like to pray?

—Yes, he whispered.

He drank in each word of these two prayers and his eyes were amazingly clear. The cancer had spread throughout his body and the doctors wanted to try chemotherapy. The Lord took him. *Ouf!*

–I want to return to the Companions, he said.

After talking it over with Pierre, we realized it wasn't possible.

–You'll go home, to your own house, I promise you.

I wasn't lying when I said that, because we had often asked Jesus to take him home to his eternity.

That evening, in the chapel of the Companions, one other Companion and I. We pray before the Blessed Sacrament exposed. I relax in his presence and a feeling of calm gently overtakes me.

–Your eternity, Jesus. What is your eternity?

–*Me.*

–What do you mean?

–*Look at me.*

I do so, and at *that moment* the host is a living man with wide-open arms who speaks to me. This isn't the result of my impressionability or my imagination. It cuts *straight to the heart.*

–I see you, my Lord and my God. What love, dear Jesus.

At a time when I'm not at all expecting it, here he is, flooding me with his tenderness. I savor this moment because he's here, speaking to me. It's not that he returned, because he never left. But now he's *here,* speaking to me. I weep for joy.

–Thank you, Lord. I needed this time so much.

–*I'll never abandon you, I promise you. It's been rough and it will continue to be that way, but I have chosen you, little sister, little queen, my queen, the queen of my heart.*

–I believe you. Yes, I believe you, and at this very moment I want to tell everyone about you at the top of my lungs.

–*There will be a time for that. Don't be impatient. I've already told you so.*

A few moments later:

–Jesus, let's get back to what we were talking about. What about your eternity?

–It is I, in this moment, but even greater and more all-encompassing. There is no break. Do you understand?

–Yes.

Saturday, December 10

Philippe has to go to Lyons on business, and I'm going along for a couple of days of rest. It's good to slow down and simply live. The return to Chartres is difficult. One of the volunteers who helped us considerably two years ago has turned out to be a big-time swindler. Suddenly the Companions and I are the talk of the town. We are front-page news in a local paper and become the focal point of a mess that attracts the scandalmongers. I can hardly believe the suspicions and questions that are directed at me, and I have to deal with people who are delighted to pick up the scent of a scandal in the making. An anonymous telephone call insinuating horrible things infuriates me. I'm physically beat and emotionally disgusted. It's not just the evil in itself that angers me; I am dumbfounded by the willingness of these poor souls to wallow in it, or to fabricate a rotten affair out of it.

Sunday evening, alone at home, my tears gush forth.

I entrust to Mary everything that I have discovered and have had to live through:

–Mary, this wickedness, these demons: take them all, bind them to the foot of the cross of your Son. Protect us, protect me from their attacks. Protect the Community, the little ones. Mary, Mary. I don't have any more strength. . . .

Calm returns.

Monday, December 12 (mass at the chapel)

—I will make you a queen. I am making you a queen. My queen, don't be afraid of anything.

—Oh, Jesus, look at this mess – your humanity, our efforts. . . . I'm a pretty sorry queen.

—Not at all. You're beautiful. You are a queen, my queen.

—What are you doing now? What do you want of me? Surely you can see what I'm going through?

—I'm building the pedestal together with you.

—The pedestal?

—Yes, the pedestal for the queen, in order to lift you up a little bit, Nicole, and allow you to be seen.

—The pedestal? I don't understand.

—You have overcome evil, Nicole. In order to overcome it, you had to meet it head-on. It's over. Like me, you have overcome it.

—Jesus.

It's a cry that comes from my whole being.

I don't resist. I know that I have overcome. I breathe deeply before resuming the dialogue.

—I believe you. It was quite a battle, but I know that I've won. It's enough to make me feel arrogant. Perhaps I'm being a little arrogant in telling you that I won.

—No. As long as you fight together with me, as long as you leave me some room, you won't become arrogant.

Friday, December 16

I talk to him once again about the queen, his "little queen."

—I, too, give witness, Nicole.

—But you don't have to give witness. You have already given it, the witness only you could give.

—I am alive. I give witness by making you a queen.

—The two of us give witness together, is that it?

—Yes.

—And my witness?

—Be at peace. Don't be afraid of anything. Show your joy.

A little later:

—I'll take care of everything. Don't worry about it. I'll see to everything.

—It's hard for me to believe you in the middle of this crazy mess.

—I'll do it.

—I believe you.

I have the impression that Jesus wants me to adhere to him totally, even though I may not know what he's going to do in this kingdom he's fashioning. Peace and trust are the part I have to play.

—May your will be done, Jesus. I'm in your hands. I'll try to be completely at peace. But you must know, Jesus, how these anonymous telephone calls upset me. So please give me a little time between calls to get myself together again.

—I am your protector. They won't do anything to you. Be at peace.

December

For several months now I have been noticing that it's easier for me to meet Jesus when I'm alone, whether at mass or elsewhere. I've often wondered if this is simply because I'm too self-centered. I'd like to see myself a little more clearly. I'm alone in the car, driving to the Hermitage.

—Jesus? Is it I who am too self-centered or might you perhaps be a little jealous?

—Yes, I am a little jealous.

Boom. My heart goes "boom."

–You? Jealous?

–*Yes. When we talk to each other, Nicole, it's important that you give yourself to me completely.*

–You? Jealous?

It's still hard for me to accept these words.

–*Yes, yes. To give you more and to live in you more. Afterwards you'll only be richer because of this, richer for the others. Nicole, I really am a living person.*

End of December

These have been difficult and trying days. My soul feels fogged in and weighed down. I have the impression that someone is going through a very difficult time. About all I can do is pray without really understanding what's going on.

January 1989 (mass at the Companions)

–*Rejoice, Nicole. Rejoice.*

–It's "Rejoice, Mary," not Nicole. I've misunderstood, Jesus.

–*No. Rejoice, Nicole.*

A passing moment of uncertainty, but there is such a sense of peace in my heart that I know this isn't an invention of my imagination.

–*I'll gladden your heart again, for my kingdom.*

–I believe you, Lord.

Sunday (mass at Saint Aignan)

Isaiah 62:4. "You shall be called My Delight Is in Her, and your land Married."

These words go right to my heart, as if they were spoken to me. It's crazy.

–I already have a husband. You gave him to me, Jesus.

–*Yes.*

The Lord is in front of me, enfolding me.

–*I wed not only your being, but your whole life, your family. It's even greater than that. The you I wed includes all the experiences I give you.*

The Gospel of the wedding at Cana.

–*Do what she did.*

After thinking about this for a moment, I ask him:

–You want me to act as she did? Mary lives on two levels at the same time. There's the human predicament of running out of wine and the fact that you're divine. Mary knows that you can do something about it. She doesn't know what, but she trusts that you'll act.

–*Yes, Nicole.*

–You want me to do what she did. I'm to live out whatever you give me to live out, without reserve, and I'm to trust you without knowing how you're going to respond when I call to you.

–*Yes.*

I meditate and pray a little.

–Jesus, there's something that just doesn't seem right: it's too simple.

–*My love is simple. You make it all so complicated.*

–But in a relationship, there's a give-and-take. What am I supposed to do? I can't just receive and let myself be led.

At that very moment the priest speaks about the "feeble participation" that God asks of us when he works a miracle. He gives the example of the bread and the fish. It's so little, and the crowd is so huge.

–I do want to participate, Lord. So what can I give? What do you want of me?

–*Your spirit. Nicole. I have already told you that. The spirit that leads you to go out to others, to me. Your vibrant spirit.*

–That's not very hard. I'm happy to give it to you. What else?

–*Your trust. Like Mary, your trust. Your childlike trust, which knows that I'm going to do something but isn't concerned about the how.*

–That will surely be more difficult at times, but I'll do my best. I promise you. We'll work together; you have my word.

–*I want them to see me, to know that I am alive.*

Several times during the mass I'm shocked to hear:

–*My Father will come to visit you.*

–To speak to me?

–*Yes.*

I tell Pierre about this because I'm so surprised by these words that I'm afraid I'm losing my grip.

–Write it down, Pierre tells me.

He doesn't seem to be at all surprised. We'll see.

13

0

Do What My Son Did

Here I am, suddenly transported to another planet. I leave home and the Companions and now am with eight rich and spoiled Americans on a two-week camel trip in the desert. Assekrem, Charles de Foucauld's sanctuary, is so beautiful it takes my breath away. I leave my little notebook with the brothers at Foucauld's hermitage. I feel both intimidated and stupid when I tell Father Georges what it's about. He doesn't seem in the least surprised. *Insh Allah.* If God so wills.

Two days by car. I let myself be rocked and I dream. It hurts me to feel far away from Jesus. I put away my daydreaming and tell him so.

–*Leave your artificial paradise, your daydreaming.*

I do so and enter into the silence.

–I feel a great emptiness, Jesus. Not only the emptiness of the surroundings, but a great emptiness between you and me.

–*Live in my presence.*

–But the emptiness is empty, Jesus.

–*No.*

–What do you mean, no?

–*This emptiness that you feel isn't empty. It's the bond between my Father and his creation. Live in it with your prayers, like the brothers of the Assekrem hermitage.*

Yes. Like them on their high plateau, between heaven and earth.

January 31

–Explain this inhabited emptiness.

–*You're weaving together with my Father.*

–Weaving what?

–*Why do you want to know?*

–Why, in order to know.

–*Know what? What good will that do?*

February 1 (still in the desert)

–Tell me about this weaving, Jesus.

–*It's prayer to my Father, toward my Father, with him.*

–How is he different from you?

–*I am your companion. I go before you. I'm in day-to-day life.*

–And your Father?

–*Include the universe, the immensity of the world, in your prayer.*

–Now, Jesus, I honestly don't think that is going to change anything, whether it's in Chile, in the USSR, in Lebanon, or anywhere else. Just take a look at the chaos.

—Let your prayer be completely disinterested.

—What do you mean?

—Pray to enter into a relationship, without self-will. The same for the people I have given you. Don't pray to convert them or to reform them. Just pray for them.

—I understand.

—Be like my Son.

This time it's God who speaks. (I'm so frightened I hardly have the courage to write these words.)

—Like your Son?

—Think about the cross.

—Yes, you're right. He prayed for his persecutors. He didn't pray that his persecutors would stop doing what they were doing. Yes, I understand.

And later:

—How should I refer to you?

—By my name.

—Well then, God, I'm going to dare to ask you this question. It may be stupid, but you initiated this conversation. What's the use, or better, what use is it for me to pray for a world and for situations that are completely beyond me? Here I am, lost in your universe. My brothers are swallowed up in your universe. It's crazy. And furthermore, I don't see anything, don't know anything.

—Pray. First of all, you will enter into relationship with me. That will provide you with a way of entering into the vestibule of my eternity.

I have time to meditate on this as we walk in the Teffedest. But I'm still astounded. It's at once so immense and so simple.

February 2

—God, you gave us our intelligence so that we could understand. You're the one who wanted it that way. So

then, you who are the Alpha and the Omega, you who have sent your Son to the world, take a look for yourself. The world is in trouble; it's a mess. Your Son died for us, but nothing under the sun has changed. What's the use? How do you expect people to believe in you? You know it's hard. We don't understand anything at all about your plan.

—Understanding my plan is not the point. I'm only asking you and all the others to contribute to it.

—So I have to put my intelligence on hold, on the back burner?

—No. Just submit your intelligence to a plan that you don't understand because you will never be able to understand it completely.

—Partly, then?

—Yes, but just a little bit.

—What do you want of us?

—Contribute to my plan with what you have and from where you stand. That's all.

February 3

—It's absurd. We really are nothing at all. I am nothing. A little grain of sand in this vast stretch of sand. Nothing. Minuscule. It's really quite ridiculous, isn't it?

—Yes. You're this little nothing, this grain of sand.

—Nothing. It's hard for me to accept that.

—In this nothing, there is everything. My All. There is me.

February 4

—How do we comprehend, how do we live and accept being nothing at all?

—With gentleness, patience, and modesty.

–What do you mean?

–*Like a work of art.*

–What do you mean?

–*A work of art retains its secret, its mystery. Do the same for my universe, my plan. Treat it like a work of art. Accept that there's more to it than you can understand.*

Sunday, February 5

–A work of art. I don't like that. All these people, all these evils, all these distortions. How can you call it a work of art when there are so many disasters, such unhappiness, the death of innocent children? It's impossible.

–*My work of art is not finished. It is still going on.*

I think, of course, of Teilhard de Chardin.

–*Do what my Son did.*

–What do you mean?

–*Live as he lived. He was just the son of a carpenter in a little village. Live as he lived where you are, and like him, carry the world. Don't look for anything beyond being small, the mother of a family, the person who today is responsible for the Community.*

–That's what you want of me?

–*That is what we want of you today.*

February 6

–A work of art, with so much suffering? Misfortune, the suicide of a child . . . so much tragedy. I know, lots of books have been written, so much has been said about suffering, but what about the look of a person who is suffering? God, you're all-knowing. Can you give me an answer, a simple answer?

—I share it.

—What do you mean?

—I am in the suffering, in the look, in the agony.

—But, God, you need two to share. All those who don't know you are unable to share and don't know that you are sharing with them.

—Nonetheless, I am there.

—But what good is that for them, since they aren't aware of it? Since they can't feel anything, it's no help to them.

—What makes you so sure of that? Don't put yourself in their place. Once and for all my Son put himself in their place. He bore everything.

February 7

—We have to put up with all this suffering.

—No. What you have to do is direct it toward us, and to do so with all your strength.

February 9 (back at Tamanrasset)

I go to see the Little Sisters and listen to a talk on Charles de Foucauld.

Here I am all by myself, kneeling in the little chapel of the sisters. I have my feet in the sand, as I did in the desert. The presence of Jesus in the tabernacle makes me feel warm inside.

I think about Charles de Foucauld and his remarkable life.

—Did anything come of it? Do you want the same thing to happen to us, to me?

—Carry the world.

—But it's absurd. Why use me? What can I accomplish? What do you want me to do?

–*Nothing.*

–What do you mean?

–*Why do you always want to do something? Aren't you already busy enough? Why do you want to do more?*

–Then what do you want of me?

–*Don't do anything. Let us do it.*

–That's incomprehensible.

–*No, it's not.*

–What ought I to do – or rather, since we're not talking about doing, what ought I to be?

–*Carry us in yourself.*

–That's all?

–*Yes. Like two treasures nestled down deep inside you. That's all.*

February 10

–God, it's so simple. What you're saying is that we complicate everything, even those who think they're following you?

–*Yes. My son and I are worn out by your useless efforts.*

–What do you mean?

–*You put so much effort into living your lives and carrying out your projects that you leave no room for us.*

–The spirit of childhood, is that it? To trust completely and let oneself be led?

–*Yes.*

February 12 (the airport at Algiers)

–Along with the joy of knowing you, there is always the cross.

–*Yes.*

–Joy and the cross, always?

–*Yes.*

–I'm afraid of the cross.

–*Don't be afraid of it.*

–How can one not be afraid, not fear it? It seems to me that you ask a lot of those you have chosen.

–*No.*

–What do you mean?

–*The cross will not be heavy, because we will carry it along with you. We protect you. No one will be able to harm you. Believe it. Like a child, believe it.*

–It's easier than I imagine?

–*It is even easier than the life you are now leading.*

–??!! Easier?

–*Yes, because you really have no idea how much we surround you with our love.*

–Really chosen?

–*Yes.*

I'm reminded again, both in my head and in my heart, of the "spirit of childhood" so dear to Bernanos, the poverty of Foucauld, the humility of Teilhard, and of so many others, both known and unknown.

February 13 (back home)

Far from the silence and the beauty of the desert, I return once again to the intimacy of the family. I have the impression that passing from one planet to another has become less difficult. Probably it's because I'm letting go more than I did before.

February 15

–Why do you insist so much that we not do anything?

–*When you become too active, you don't let our presence shine through.*

Sunday, February 20 (mass at Saint Aignan)

In his homily the pastor speaks insistently about two worlds: the present, ephemeral world, and the true world that awaits us after our death.

–That's difficult for me to accept. I feel as if I'm being torn in two. I love this life here below, and I don't believe enough in the life that awaits me. The eternity that we will tumble into is hazy and vague. I'd like to believe more strongly, to be convinced in the depth of my being that joy awaits me. But you know how far I am from that.

–*Don't try to imagine it. You're unable to know it. Besides, you're mistaken.*

–?

–*There is no before and after. There is only the present – today, right now.*

–Eternity has already begun?

–*Yes, of course.*

A few moments later:

–How do we live this eternity, this today? It's difficult, isn't it? When I'm making dinner, talking, reading a book – in short, when I'm doing the hundred and one things that make up this daily life, I can't be with you at the same time. Not all the time. It's impossible.

–*Simply leave the door of your heart open to our presence. Do what you're doing completely and well.*

–And you?

–*Once in a while we'll come and surprise you. We'll meet each other.*

February

A strong impression of the presence of Jesus. He even asks me,

–*How is it going, Nicole?* just as a friend would do. And then he continues:

–*Don't worry about anything. None of you needs to worry about anything. Make your ways smooth.*

–You mean to say that we should make the way smooth for you?

–*No. Simplify your lives. What I'm sending you are just a few rough spots.*

Sunday, February 26 (mass at Saint Aignan)

–I'd like to enter into your eternity serenely, just as I'm living now. That seems difficult.

–*No.*

–What do you mean?

–*Turn the movement around. Don't start from what you don't know, are unable to know. Don't start from what you imagine or fear after death. Start from what you see today.*

April 25

A telephone call this morning from someone who asks me to pray for her. She wants to remain anonymous. The simplicity and the tension in her voice affect me deeply. I promise that Pierre will offer mass for her and that we will carry her in our hearts. The same day I receive a radiant letter from a friend of Uncle André who read my little notebook. She has cancer and is undergoing chemotherapy. She tells me how much the notebook is helping her. The letter is radiant because it reveals the nobility of a great soul, just like that of Thérèse. What a gift it is to be able to share on this level.

This evening at mass I offer him these two souls and I feel profoundly heavy and sad. I confide their suffer-

ings to him and enter into a kind of somber universe: calm but somber.

–It's difficult, Jesus, so difficult.

–*I know.*

I can physically sense that he knows. The words of the Gospel come to me. I mutter to myself:

–It just doesn't work, Jesus. You know what we need, you know better than anyone else, and yet you want us to ask you for it. And so we ask you and at the same time we say, "Thy will be done."

I have the impression, ridiculous perhaps, that we are playing with loaded dice.

–*Pray, Nicole, pray.*

–To what purpose? You know that I can't do anything as well as you can. To what purpose?

–*Your prayer will make my collaboration with these two souls even greater. Do you understand?*

–Do you mean that my prayer draws you closer?

–*Yes. Do you believe that?*

–Yes. I believe you.

Summer (Finland)

A family vacation with a friend. Everyone unwinds. Way out on an island without running water or electricity, we have the time to let the hours roll by. I was hoping that we would meet each other.

–Aren't you going to come and see me anymore?

"*Relax*" was all I heard.

And so I relaxed.

August

No encounters. I miss them. I tell them so.

–You come without warning, you go away without letting me know, and you leave me high and dry. It's

difficult to accept this silence without any explanation. Moreover, as you well know, I feel like a post stuck in the middle of the road. I feel heavy and no longer experience the sweet delight of your presence. That's rather hard to accept.

—Don't get upset. We're molding you. We know better than you what you need. We're not far away from you. You are our queen.

So be it.

I accept their apparent absence.

On several occasions, as the host is being elevated, I see the face of Jesus. In the beginning it looked like the face on the Holy Shroud and I told myself it was an optical illusion. But my overwhelming feeling of calm assures me that it is not a mirage.

14

०

The Time Has Come for Us to Act

December 1989

Is this the sequel to the little notebook? I don't know. I really am letting go. Jesus has not abandoned me, but it's more than two months now that I have been without these moments of eternity. What I feel so deeply is not his absence but his distance. I accept it, but it's not easy. Since the initiative is his, there's really nothing I can do, but at mass I often ask him to return.

—You've spoiled me a lot, I know. You asked me to put this little notebook into practice, and to integrate it into my life. I'm trying. But, if it be your will, come and visit me. If it's not your will, I accept that.

He came back on Thursday. Of course, I begged him to, but that's my way of holding on to the relationship.

Kneeling, he takes me in his arms and surrounds me with such love that I'm almost out of breath.

—Now are you reassured?

—Yes. Can't you tell?

—I am alive.

I savor these moments, astounded and also profoundly happy. I believe that if the world came to an end at this moment I'd be happy about it. I feel permeated through and through by an inner peace.

—This is what is waiting for you in my eternity. This is my eternity.

I can honestly say that if that's what eternity is like, I'd be perfectly willing to die right now.

—Don't be afraid. What I say to you, I say to all of you. Don't be afraid.

And later:

—I have chosen you. You are my queen.

—Yes, Jesus. You're starting all over again. It's too much, too beautiful for me. Set me down where I belong.

—No. Nothing is too much for my kingdom. I have chosen you.

The next day: Friday.

—Move easily, Nicole, move easily.

—Move easily? What do you mean by that?

—Move easily among the people that I give you, among all the events I have put into your life. Don't linger over them.

—Why? Tell me what you mean.

—Move easily and you'll become light, peaceful, beautiful. Don't do anything. I'll act in your place. Let me act.

—You have chosen me to do nothing?

—Yes.

—Then I'm of no use?

—I will make use of you.

—Tell me what you mean, Jesus. Tell me what you mean.

—I love you.

There I am, literally swallowed up in this love. It's almost too much for me. I tell him so.

—Let me tell you something, Jesus. I have missed you all this time, and now that you talk to me like this, I feel almost afraid of this immense love. It makes me feel faint, Jesus.

—Yes, I know.

—You want me to let go.

—Yes.

I'm going to try. It's not all that difficult, and yet it baffles me.

Wednesday, February 7, 1990

All alone, I stop off at a little Romanesque chapel at La Grave in the southern Alps.

I speak to them.

—Your silence is a bit long and heavy. You don't speak to me anymore. I miss you.

Silence.

I insist. A reply:

—We already told you. We know what's good for you. We're taking care of you in other ways.

And it's true. I feel that help has never been lacking with the Companions. It's as if every time there was some need, they gave me the right person for the job.

—It's true. I know I've been spoiled, even though I didn't deserve it, but I still miss you. Why this silence?

—In order to shape you. We are shaping you.

—What for?

—So that you may resemble my Son.

It is God who speaks, and this time I feel much less intimidated.

—I'll never make it.

—No, you won't. But we will.

—So what I have to do is let go, accepting even this silence.

—Yes.

Friday, February 9

Still at La Grave. Philippe is skiing slopes that are too difficult for me. I return to the chapel to see them, but this time it's locked. Too bad! I sit down on one of the steps in front of the cemetery and gaze at the Meije peak. The sun bathes the frosted cemetery and I'm surrounded by the silence.

—Thank you. This is beautiful.

And a little later:

—How are you shaping me? And for what purpose?

—Because you have to enter into the depths of silence.

—I'm a little afraid of silence. It's empty. It doesn't speak to me.

—No. Our silence.

—What do you mean?

—We are inside the silence. With you, inside *the silence.*

—But without speaking to me? Why?

—Adoration, Nicole. This silence, our silence. We speak to you in a different way. Enter into adoration.

—What do you want me to do?

—Nothing.

—But how am I to adore you?

—By letting go. Don't do anything. It's we who dwell in the silence, not you.

—All I have to do is make room for you?

—Yes.

And it's true that they're there, both of them, and all I have to do is close my eyes to enter into my soul. I go

down into it and they're there waiting for me, both of them.

I'm no longer afraid of God. It's terribly simple. The Father and the Son and . . . me.

–It's simple, very simple, too simple.

–People make everything so complicated.

–Wait a minute. Experiencing your presence right now, it's easy for me. What about the others, those other men and women, some of them in religious life, who struggle with doubt and emptiness?

–Once again you're complicating everything. At this moment we're not talking about the others, but about you.

–No, you're not going to put me off so easily. I have been blessed a thousand times over. You fell on my soul without warning and you made it your dwelling, while others who have given *everything* to you never find you.

–We have already given you an answer.

–You did?

–We have inscribed these people on your heart. We already told you that.

–What about Thérèse? All I have to do is keep her in my heart?

–Yes. We'll take care of her.

–Good.

February 17 (on the way to the Community)

For some time now the word *lamb* has been on my mind.

–Lamb? What are you trying to tell me?

–That is the way to meet us.

–What do you mean?

–The man or woman who has been a "lamb," an "innocent one" in life, is able to meet us.

–Is it necessary to have experienced this trial in order to know you?

–*Yes. You either have to have experienced it yourself or through others.*

–That's the only way?

–*That is where we meet.*

–How difficult it is. We have to be bruised to talk with you. It's crazy.

The beginning of March

I speak to them.

–"Don't judge." That annoys me. How can we not judge? Like it or not, there is always light and shadow. To say "Everything is fine, everything is just perfect" isn't only false. An attitude like that can be dangerous or idiotic.

–*Yes, you're right. Of course it's necessary to judge deeds. But never imprison people in their deeds, never hold them there.*

–What do you mean?

–*You are all in the process of becoming. Let's say you just noticed that someone has committed an offense. Fine. But look at the person and recognize that sometime in the future, sooner or later, that person will be able to choose the light.*

–So I leave an opening. Is that what you mean?

–*No, you do more. You allow us to act with you. To look at these people with you, to understand them, to wait for them with you. Do you understand?*

–Yes. What it comes down to is that I'm giving you a chance as well!

March 8 (the chapel of the Companions)

The host is in our hands: fragile, vulnerable.

I say to them:

—You're so light and vulnerable in my hand. It's crazy.

I meditate a little on this piece of bread that is Jesus.

I hear:

—*Be light. I want you to be as light as I am right now.*

Since I'm not really sure that it's he who is speaking to me, I wait a little. There is peace. So it is he, and not my wishing it or my imagination.

—Will you tell me what you mean? Maybe tomorrow?

—*Yes.*

The next day, March 9

I have some time for tidying up the house, and since I'm alone we speak to one another.

—Can you tell me what you mean by light? And explain vulnerable, too. That word is a little scary.

—*Yes, light. As for vulnerable, don't be afraid. You know that we are protecting you.*

—Why light?

—*Don't carry what you don't have to carry. It's too heavy for you. You're not up to it.*

I don't agree and I tell them so:

—You created me, brought me into this world with my talents and flaws. To give an example, I was born with a certain degree of understanding and compassion. They were your gifts. And now I'm to put all this aside?

—*No. Do you think that we forgot about you the day after you were born? We are there at your side.*

—How does lightness fit in?

—*We are at your side. You feel, you see, you sympathize, but let us carry what is too heavy for you. Be light. We will do the carrying and they will see us.*

–They?

–*The people that we give you, that we lend you. The lighter you are, the more they will see us.*

March (on the way to the Companions)

–I have the impression that you're trying to get me to live on two different planets. The first is that of the "hidden kingdom": your presence, the little notebook, the little miracles that you let me experience. The second is that of the world: the thousand and one things that make up our daily life, the major and minor decisions (and there are plenty of them), and all that weighs down our human existence. I feel tossed from one to the other, and it doesn't feel very good. And why? Why the intimacy, the secrecy, of the kingdom?

–*So that you don't distort it.*

–What do you mean? Why isn't this hidden kingdom revealed to everyone?

–*In order that the "little" may nourish the "great." In order that the intimacy of the little notebook may nourish your life. You have to begin with us so that our kingdom may break forth.*

I understand. Yes, I think I understand.

The next day

–You know everything about me. Everything, from all eternity. And yet you allow me to be free to choose to love or not to love. Even before I open my mouth, you know what I'm going to ask you. What a strange and yet provocative kind of liberty this is: determined and free at the same time!

–*Yes, we know everything, Nicole. But* in a completely different way, *not in your way. Neither your intelligence*

nor any human intelligence can know as we know. Our way of knowing is not the human way.

—What then is the link or the means by which we can catch a glimpse of you? There has to be one.

—*Trust.*

—Nothing else?

—*No.*

— . . .

—To trust in you in the dark, without knowing.

—*Yes, but not in the dark.*

—Why is that?

—*Because it is through trust that we enter into a relationship with you. It is the* relationship *that we desire.*

—But what about all those who never experience this relationship? What about all the prayers that have gone unanswered?

—*Our answers are not your answers. You want us to answer you in* your *way. At times, our answers can be completely different.*

—But then would we ever be able to understand them or even receive them?

—*Yes, but often it comes about gradually.*

I still have some questions to ask later. But first of all I have to assimilate what they're trying to get me to understand.

Very often I see a face coming into focus on the host when it's elevated. Sometimes it looks like the face on the Holy Shroud, and at other times the face is inclined. The gaze directed toward me comes from far, far away, but it's still very close. I've already experienced something of this same feeling of sweetness when I've been embraced by the gaze of some people. That has happened rarely, very rarely, but the feeling is one of extreme sweetness.

I remain calm. I feel neither dizziness nor doubt, and when I don't see him on the host, I'm not bothered

by it because I know that he's there. It's all so simple and straightforward, but I'm still surprised by how calm I am. "Let go." Okay. I am letting go.

March 28

For a couple of days now I have wanted to ask which requests are good, and which bad. "Ask and you shall receive." I feel like replying, Not always!

Several times I ask them:

–What are the good requests?

I know that they will answer me. I wait for the right moment.

After Communion, as I'm thanking them for the life they give me, the answer comes:

–*The good requests are those that come from your heart.*

–And the bad?

–*Those that come from your plans.*

–So what you want more than anything else is heart-to-heart?

–*Yes.*

April (Paris)

Paris is a bit like Sodom and Gomorrah. Everything is possible, everything is permitted in the name of a pseudoliberty and of a so-called truth. I can't help feeling sick at heart. I don't want to take the *métro,* so I walk for over an hour. That gives us time to talk. And, as is always the case when I'm feeling upset, the same thought comes to my mind.

–Look around you, Jesus. You came into our world. This is Holy Week, and you're about to go to your cross. You're going to take everything up into your cry of agony. But what a mess this is!

There it is. I'd like to be consoled by him who is still suffering. I insist:

—Don't tell me, Jesus, that this is just something between you and me. I see the others. I see how they're suffering. I hear them splashing around as they sink deeper and deeper. Look at them. Take a close look at them.

—*I know, Nicole. I know everything. But I did not come to be a reformer.*

—What do you mean?

—*Be like me, don't try to reform them. You wouldn't succeed anyway.*

—Be like you? What do you mean?

—*Carry them in your heart. Place them deep within your heart, in the emptiness of your tears, and, like me, wait.*

—Wait for what?

—*Their conversion.*

—Once more, I don't have to do anything, just wait?

—*Yes.*

—Will you wait with me?

—*Of course. Don't do anything. I'll take care of it.*

December (In the Alps. A ski lodge at Chamonix)

Five free days. It's cold and snowy, but I'm with Philippe, the sun peeks out now and then, and there's a little church not too far away.

Finally I'm able to slow down, and since I'm often by myself, I go to see him each day in the church of Agentière. It's cold, and I don't especially care for the gold-encrusted baroque altar. You'd think you were in Austria. I'm taken aback, as I was in Patmos, by this "dripping" display of affluence. Jesus was born in a stable, after all.

For a long time now I have been wondering about sin and about myself. It seems to me that I have become

reconciled with sin. I don't feel any guilt; at least I don't feel it anymore. Whenever I feel I have offended someone, I find a way to apologize as soon as possible. So where am I? Am I being proud, or is it just that my understanding of a basic Christian concept is lacking?

I talk to him best when I'm walking.

–This is day number two that I have come to see you, both of you, in your gilded church. Would you like to enlighten me?

Deep down I know that he will answer me, and at the same time, I know that he will answer me in his own good time.

I know that sin is serious, that sins are serious, and yet I don't feel in any way burdened with sin.

–Am I being proud? Or am I totally mistaken?

The answer finally comes on the third day.

–*Sin is like prayer.*

I try to understand.

–Tell me what you mean.

–*When you pray, you speak to me. You enter into a relationship with me. When you confess your sins, that, too, is a way of speaking to me.*

–Jesus, for me sin is believing that we are God, that we are all-powerful. I don't think I do that. I'm pretty well aware of my limits, but I'm not very burdened by them. What good does it do to talk about them in confession, or even to mention them to you directly?

–*It's better when you say them.*

–What's better?

–*Our relationship. The hidden kingdom.*

–What do you mean?

–*When you tell me about your limits, you enter into a relationship with me and you hand these limits over to me. Do you understand?*

–If I hand my limits over to you, if I tell you about them, then you'll be able to "do" something with them?

–*Yes. You allow me to act, to extend you. You know what I'm talking about; you have already experienced it: we are two. You do your human work and I extend it; I extend you.*

–So it's not something negative.

–*No, not at all.*

My remark seems to make him smile.

February–March 1991

It's neither absence nor silence. Nor is it the night. And yet . . . This friend that I was meeting so regularly has all of a sudden disappeared.

–We aren't in Lent any longer.

No answer.

–As you like, whenever you like, but it's so good when you come to speak to me.

No answer.

One day, in my exasperation, I say to him:

–Is it because I'm not humble enough that you don't come back anymore?

–*I didn't come to visit you because of your humility.*

Bang! So much for me!

There are days when I say "As you like, whenever you like" and actually mean it and feel at peace about it. And there are others when I'm really irritated.

An evening at the Hermitage during the Eucharist

–You're too much for me, Jesus. You come when I'm not expecting it. You make your dwelling in me when I haven't even invited you, and all of a sudden you're

gone without giving any warning. It's a little too casual for my taste.

I have to enter into myself and be silent in order finally to receive his reply.

—I will show you other "landscapes."

—Without you?

—No, with me, but in a different way.

And I know what he means: At the Community when Pierre is gone and in my own home I sometimes marvel at the way his kingdom is being fashioned. It's not very obvious, and yet it's very strong. For example, the tensions among the members of the Community that are suddenly resolved even though Pierre is not around. It's true that when I'm all by myself with these men, I do let go when I see that there is nothing more that I can do.

I'm often surprised to find myself saying, "You can take care of this or that yourself." It's quick and off-the-cuff, but it works. At any rate, I can't pick up an army cot and move into the Community!

—It's true, I feel you at work all around me, even though I had nothing to do with it.

—That's what I promised you.

—Are you really going to take me along with you?

—Yes.

March

I had the impression a couple of nights ago that the devil was prowling around me. I confess a certain reserve toward those who talk about devils. I'm sure they exist, but I think it's dangerous to see them everywhere. I believe it's better to live out fully the humanity that Jesus has molded for us and not worry about the world of angels and devils. Still, I have to recognize that I may

be mistaken. Sometimes I can sense in certain souls a rigidity so strong that it seems to be made of concrete. I'm almost ready to give a name to what's troubling them or causing their disequilibrium. I refrain from saying anything, of course, but at times I feel my heart begin to beat faster. It doesn't last long, but it comes on me suddenly and it's very strong, as if it were caused by something "outside" of me. When it happens, I immediately pray to Mary and my heart stops pounding.

The other night, when I was home alone, I think I physically sensed the presence of the devil. After having spent an hour in prayer with Pierre and the Bon Secours sisters, I finally came home, happy to be able to sleep in peace in an empty house. I woke up in the middle of the night. Since I couldn't go back to sleep, I got up, walked around a bit, and then went back to bed. Suddenly I woke up with a start because I had just felt some kind of animal move over me. I instinctively reached out to grab it, but nothing was there. It was a lot stronger than a dream, and I was revolted and terrified by some slimy thing that I had physically felt crawling over me. What most surprised me, however, was that in spite of my anxiety and the moment of terror I felt when I awoke, *I was not afraid.* In some way, it didn't concern me directly.

–Mary, protect me.

I went right back to sleep. I waited several days before telling Pierre about it. The memory is very vivid, but not at all terrifying.

April

"And the angel left her." I hear these words directed to me.

–Is this the end of the little notebook, Lord?

—I have already given you much.

I have the impression that this is the end of the little notebook.

Mass at Saint Aignan

The silence weighs down on me. The "felt" presence of Jesus isn't there any longer. It's not the night, but nonetheless . . . Once more I implore him and I tell him this.

And then he comes and enfolds me.

—I will not abandon you. I have given you the little notebook so that I myself might nourish you. Now you can continue by yourself.

*—*And you?

—I will be with you, but in another way.

*—*I'd like you to be with me as I continue on.

—You're strong enough now. But you already know that.

*—*Yes, it's true. Why are you letting me continue on all by myself?

—Because those who notice this power are going to wonder where it comes from. The power that I'm giving you is going to send them to me. Do you understand?

*—*Yes.

—Then continue on by yourself.

I'd need much more time to recount all the things and the encounters that come about partly (and sometimes largely) through my intermediaries. Without my trying to program things or stand at anybody's elbow, the right persons are there and what needs to be done is done. It all happens naturally. It seems to me that all I have to do is let the current of this little notebook flow out. It's natural and in a way so easy and simple.

I have a much easier time dealing with tensions. I'm more levelheaded, and I clothe my sadness or my suf-

fering with Jesus in a way that's almost physical. The difficulties of the moment aren't taken away, but deep down within me there's a center of peace. It's new and powerful.

May–June

    —The time has come for us to act – that is what we promised you.

The Little Notebook

❍